P9-DXN-163

CAMPOBELLO

CAMPOBELLO

The outer island

by Alden Nowlan

DISCARD

CCC LIBRARY

CLARKE, IRWIN & COMPANY LIMITED
TORONTO, VANCOUVER

Copyright © 1975 by Clarke, Irwin & Company Limited

All rights reserved. No part of this publication may be reproduced or transmitted in any form or by any means, electronic or mechanical, including photocopying, recording, or any information storage and retrieval system, without permission in writing from the publisher.

This edition published in 1993 by
Stoddart Publishing Co. Limited
34 Lesmill Road
Toronto, Canada
M3B 2T6
(416) 445-3333

Canadian Cataloguing in Publication Data

Nowlan, Alden, 1933–1983.
Campobello : the outer island

ISBN 0-7737-5620-5

1. Campobello Island (N.B.) — History.   I. Title.

FC2495.C35N68 1993   971.5'33   C93-095151-4
F1044.C2N68 1993

Printed and bound in Canada

Stoddart Publishing gratefully acknowledges the support of the Canada Council, Ontario Ministry of Culture, Tourism, and Recreation, Ontario Arts Council, and Ontario Publishing Centre in the development of writing and publishing in Canada.

F
1044
.C2
N68
1975
PAP

Thanks and acknowledgments

The author gratefully acknowledges the assistance of the Canada
Horizons-Explorations Program of the Canada Council, the
co-operation of the Roosevelt Campobello International Park
Commission and its employees, and the hospitality of the people
of Campobello. For aid in conducting interviews and other
research he is indebted to David Adams Richards.

The Roosevelt Campobello Park Commission expresses its
appreciation to Mrs. Mary Gallagher for the painstaking
research which made this book possible.

    On behalf of their two governments and peoples, the
Commission expresses gratitude to the Hammer family —
Armand, Victor and Harry — for the generous gift of the
Roosevelt Cottage which made the Park possible; to the Dead
River Company for the gift of land on which the Reception
Centre is sited; and to Mr. Harry Mattin for the gift of the
Prince Cottage.

    The Commission also acknowledges the invaluable
contributions of Colonel Alexander MacNichol and Mr. Radcliffe
Pike, who have served as Executive Secretary to the Commission;
Mr. Donald Nicoll, Consultant to the Commission; Mr. Winslow
Newman, former Park Superintendent; Mr. Henry Stevens,
Park Superintendent; and the loyal and capable staff, recruited
largely from among the island people and nearby Washington
County, Maine. It is noteworthy that Mrs. Linnea Calder,

Housekeeping Supervisor, and Mr. Milton Townsend, former
gardener, also served the Roosevelt family, which is itself
represented on the Commission by their third son,
Franklin D. Roosevelt, Jr.

Preface

The interest which any place holds for us is a combination of its physical attraction — the creation of nature — and its history — the creation of the men and women who lived there. Campobello Island, whose natural and man-made attractions are extraordinary in themselves, makes a third claim on the imagination — its uniqueness as a venture in American-Canadian co-operation.

Other islands in the Bay of Fundy have air like Campobello's, so crisp one can almost shape it, so heady that to breathe it is intoxicating. Other islands off the shore of Maine and New Brunswick have soft meadows and glowing woods like those of Campobello, and vistas that embrace the solidity of the coast and the exuberance of open water. And other islands have the sudden coves, weathered piers, the look of endurance and the evidence of man's enduring.

But with all this (and more that can only be experienced, not described), the fascination of Campobello is as much symbolic as it is physical. The island William Owen settled in 1770 is now the site of the only international park in the world. It is Canadian soil which has become part of America's heritage and which is being preserved for the future through the commitment of the citizens and governments of both countries.

When Franklin Delano Roosevelt, in whose memory the

Park was created, came to Campobello as a child, it was to pursue the orderly summer adventures available to a well-to-do Victorian family. When he came as a young husband, whose third son was born on the island, it was to taste the excitements of childhood from the perspective of manhood and to pass on to his children the same challenges and rewards he had known. And finally, when he came as President of the United States, it was to take new strength and composure from Campobello's air and land, from the sea around it, and from the memories of ease his "beloved island" awoke in him.

The Roosevelt Campobello International Park, proposed by President John F. Kennedy and Prime Minister Lester B. Pearson in 1963 and officially opened in the summer of 1964 by Mrs. Lyndon B. Johnson and Mrs. Lester B. Pearson, translates all the meanings Campobello had for President Roosevelt into a living memorial. Here we remember the man and his work, his vigor and his leisure.

In 1966 President Johnson and Prime Minister Pearson laid the cornerstone for the Park Reception Center and one year later Elizabeth, the Queen Mother, officially opened the Center with the words: "It is most fitting that the memory of so gallant and industrious an American should be honored on the Canadian Island which he loved."

In the 2,600 acres of the Park at the southeast end of Campobello Island, more than a memory is preserved. The Roosevelt "cottage" is there, the simple wicker furniture and the knick-knacks of a summer home. But beyond the gardens are the bogs and the fog forests, the bays and shoals — all the natural beauties the Roosevelt family knew — protected now for others to enjoy.

The Park has grown with the acquisition of land once owned by the Campobello Company and the continuing program of restoration of cottages. As hunting and fishing are forbidden, the Park has become a bird and animal refuge. Hiking trails provide visitors with an opportunity to observe numerous species of birds and some of the most beautiful wildflowers on the continent.

And beyond preservation, the Park is acquiring the facilities to conduct small international conferences in the kind of relaxed and relaxing setting that was an essential part of the Roosevelt political style. Here men and women can examine the common issues that confront Canada and America — and all the world — with both the seriousness and the humor President Roosevelt brought to his office and its cares. Various groups, including the Premiers of the Atlantic Provinces, already have conferred there, and in 1973 Canada's Prime Minister Pierre Elliott Trudeau enjoyed a holiday in the Park, along with his wife and infant son.

Those who read this book — even if they were never to travel to Campobello — can catch in these pages the magic and the meaning of an island which is unlike any other! Although isolated by geography, it has entered the lives of two nations as a place to invite any soul and to refresh any weariness with a sense of continuity and endeavor.

The Roosevelt Campobello Park Commission congratulates the author, Alden Nowlan, for effectively placing the Park in the context of the island and its people, their history and the qualities which give them character.

Finally, the Commission dedicates this book to the people of Campobello Island. It is, after all, their island which we are privileged to share; and this is their story.

EDMUND S. MUSKIE

United States Senate
Washington, D.C.
May 1, 1975

By the same author

Bread, Wine and Salt
Miracle at Indian River
The Mysterious Naked Man
Between Tears and Laughter
Various Persons Named Kevin O'Brien
I'm a Stranger Here Myself

Contents

Prologue

Politically a part of New Brunswick, the island of Campobello is separated from the state of Maine only by a narrow tide-rip and is sixty miles by road from the Canadian mainland. It is the largest and outermost of a nest of small islands in Passamaquoddy Bay, which flows into the Bay of Fundy and is the site of some of the highest tides in the world. Since 1962 Campobello has been linked with Lubec, Maine, by the Roosevelt International Bridge, named in honour of the United States President to whom the island was a second home. It was on this wave-beaten, clift-girt island of twenty square miles, nine miles long at its longest and three miles wide at its widest, that the future President spent the summers of his boyhood and youth learning to swim, sail, hunt and fish. Here he fell victim to the poliomyelitis that permanently crippled his body but tempered his spirit.

Ever since Campobello was first settled, most of its inhabitants have lived on the eastern side of the island, near the large natural harbour called Harbour de L'Outre. There are no natural harbours on the western side; the cliffs there are higher, the area is heavily wooded and the beaches are difficult to reach. The northern and southern ends of the island provide a dramatic topographical contrast. The north, with its ledge, thin topsoil and low hills, resembles the coast of Scotland. The south is almost tropical in the luxuriance of its ferns and flowers, culminating in the Fog Forest at Liberty Point, an eerie green-gray world of lichen-hung trees shrouded in perpetual fog.

Campobello's history is unique in North America. Until 1881, when it became a summer resort for wealthy American families, such as the Roosevelts, the island was the feudal fief of a dynasty of Welsh seamen that gave the Royal Navy two admirals, one of whom was born on Campobello and the other of whom lies buried there. The first of these "Principal Proprietaries of the Great Outer Island of Passamaquoddy," Captain William Owen, landed in 1770 with a Royal Grant from King George III. When his son was born the following year he referred to him, only half-jokingly, as "the Hereditary Prince of Campobello." A later Principal Proprietary, once the tutor of the English Prime Minister William Pitt, was to describe himself, again only half-jokingly, as "both priest and king."

The Principal Proprietary was the island's lord, and the people were his tenants. His wife was given the courtesy title of Lady. He performed marriages. He prepared sermons and preached them in the church that he had caused to be built. He was inclined to regard the island's militiamen as his private army. The first Principal Proprietary erected a set of stocks and a whipping post to punish "the unruly, disorderly and dishonest," and his successors were all of them magistrates. At one point the Owens issued their own money, emblazoned with the family motto *Flecti Non Frangi* ("To be bent, not to be broken"). Of their lordship on Campobello the nineteenth-century New Brunswick historian W. F. Ganong wrote:

> It affords the best, if not the only, example of a persistence to our own day of the system under which these great grants were no doubt expected to be held, that of a large landed estate descending from father to son, with the tenants paying rent to the proprietor, as in England.

The Owen family coat of arms. Their motto — Flecti Non Frangi: "To be bent, not to be broken."

But fascinating as are the stories of the Owens and the Roosevelts it should be kept in mind that neither family touched the island so deeply nor was so deeply touched by it as the fisherfolk whose lives are largely unrecorded. Most of Campobello's 1,200 people (about 85 per cent of whom depend on fishing for their living) belong to ten families, each of which possesses its own collective identity. Island folklore says that the Newmans are absent-minded and inclined to drawl and that the Calders are born with the gift of the gab. There are similar legends about the Lanks, the Clines, the Mallochs and the others. The ancestors of some of these families were already living on the island when the first Owen sailed into Harbour de L'Outre, on the shores of which now stand the island's two villages, Wilson's Beach and Welshpool.

In the old days, Wilson's Beach belonged to the fishermen, while Welshpool identified itself with the Principal Proprie-

tary and, later, the summer people. The inhabitants of Welshpool said that the Bobbytowners of Wilson's Beach bathed in
the same tubs in which they kept the slices of herring they
used to bait their trawl-lines. The Wilson's Beach people retorted that, unlike the people of Welshpool, they did not live
on crumbs begged from rich men's tables. Today the rivalry
survives only as a running joke. When the summer people
left, early in the twentieth century, most of the islanders who
depended on them drifted away, many of them to Boston.
Now Campobello is a single community whose people speak
with an accent distinctly different from that of either the
nearby Canadian islands of Deer Island and Grand Manan or
the neighbouring Maine coast. Their speech with its broad
"a," slurred "r" and such intonations as might come from the
mouth of a Frenchman who had learned his English in Wales,

*A boy thinks long, long
thoughts on the breakwater
at Wilson's Beach.*

4

is much the same as that of their eighteenth-century ancestors. A native of Campobello could recognize another anywhere as soon as he heard him speak.

In Maine they call them Over Homers — people who say
hello to strangers and reply politely and at length to the ques-
tions of tourists who do not know a dory from a dinghy or a
cod from a pollock. But, individually and collectively, they are
private people; their world is divided into islanders and out-
siders. They are courteous and even generous to people they
do not know. But to be accepted, a newcomer must be watch-
ful and patient; he must not assume that a close acquaintance
of several months' standing is necessarily a friend. They have
inherited the strength and shrewdness of their Scots and
Yankee ancestors, but are kept from being dour by their envi-
ronment. All fishermen are gamblers — not compulsive bet-

*Welshpool. A spirited and
sometimes acrimonious
rivalry long existed between
Welshpool and Wilson's Beach,
Campobello's other village.*

tors but professional odds-players. They can never be sure whether the weather will be fair or foul, the catch good or bad, and are always conscious that when they go out in the boats it is never certain that they will come back. Forced to live with Chance, the fisherfolk of Campobello have developed a grudging affection for her.

Chapter one 🌿 The Beginning

Sweet maiden of Passamaquoddy,
Shall we seek for communion of souls
Where the deep Mississippi meanders
Or the distant Saskatchewan rolls?

Ah no! in New Brunswick we'll find it —
A sweetly sequestered nook —
Where the swift gliding Skoodawabskoosis
Unites with the Skoodawabskook.
—James DeMille

We speak of the "discovery" of America or the "discovery" of
Campobello as if nothing at all had happened on the massive
continent or the little island previous to the arrival of certain
of our European ancestors. But human beings not essentially
different from us were born, grew up, gave birth, grew old
and died in what is now New Brunswick 3,500 to 4,000 years
ago. We have opened the graves, lined with red oxide scraped
off rocks, in which they buried their dead. So it is highly
probable that men had set foot on Campobello 1,000 years or
more before the first pyramids were built in Egypt, and that
other men stood on its shores watching the sun set over Pas-

samaquoddy Bay while Moses led the Children of Israel toward the Promised Land.

Campobello was of course habitable long before the first human beings arrived there. About 15,000 years ago northwestern North America emerged from the Ice Age. The enormous ice caps that had covered the region melted. The glaciers retreated. What once had been a great valley of ice became the Bay of Fundy, and its mountain peaks were transformed into islands. Even today the waters that wash the shores of Campobello are glacial, part of that overflow from the Arctic Ocean, called the Labrador Current, that hugs the coast of North America as far south as Cape Cod, where it meets and is absorbed by the Gulf Stream. Twice each day two billion tons of icy water are carried into Passamaquoddy Bay by the tide that at its height rises twenty-nine feet.

When the Middle Ages were under way in Europe there lived in New Brunswick direct ancestors of the native peoples who still make their homes there: the Micmacs and the Maliseets. The European explorers gave them these names, as they gave the name Passamaquoddy Indians to the indigenous inhabitants of the mainland adjacent to Campobello. "Passamaquoddy" is a corruption of the Indian *pes-te-no-ka-tek,* translated as "the place where pollock abound." Pollock still abound in Passamaquoddy Bay, although not to the extent that they did during the youth of Walton Malloch. At eighty-six, this old fisherman from Wilson's Beach can remember when the pollock feeding on shrimp just below the surface of the water were so numerous that they seemed not to be separate fish but a single giant sea serpent. The island that we now know as Campobello is said to have been called *a-bah-quiet* by the Indians, which is variously translated as "parallel with the mainland," or (and this is probably more accurate), "island in the sea," as distinct from an island in a lake or river.

Walton Malloch: "I've seen the herring so thick they rolled up on the shore."

8

Life for the Passamaquoddy Indians, as for most living creatures since the beginning of time, was a constant single-minded struggle for survival. Theirs was a pre-agricultural society. They were nomads, the sole object of whose wanderings was food. In the spring and summer they came to the sea in search of fish and shellfish, and in the fall and winter they went inland again to hunt for beaver and caribou. On Campobello they dug clams, some of which they smoked, dried and skewered on sticks so that they could be carried away and used to ward off starvation during the long dark months of deep snow and freezing winds. As they returned to the island year after year, decade after decade and century after century, heaps of shells accumulated on the beaches. These heaps, at Indian Beach in the north and at Indian Point in the south, are the only surviving evidence of the passage through life of countless generations of men and women.

The Indian women made pots by scraping clay out of riverbanks, shaping it by hand, decorating it with a sharpened stick and baking it in the campfire. The men hunted and fought with stone axes, spears and arrows, and used knives made from flint or split beaver teeth. Their one great creation was the birchbark canoe; what the horse was to the Indians of the plains, the canoe was to the Indians of the east. With it they travelled the length and breadth of the Maritime Provinces and New England, and even visited the Magdalen Islands and Newfoundland.

There is a Passamaquoddy Indian legend of how, long ago, they were visited by a strange tribe called the *Caansoos*. Some researchers believe these *Caansoos* to have been Vikings. In the 1890's a Saint John, New Brunswick, newspaper published a report that the ruins of an ancient vessel with no metal in its fastenings had been found in a cove at Campobello, but evidently the discovery was never examined by an expert. The odds are that Spanish, Portuguese or French fishermen had visited the island before 1607 when it appeared, on a map drawn by the explorer Samuel de Champlain, as *Port aux Coquilles* (Isle of Clams).

A few years earlier, Champlain and Pierre du Guast, Sieur de Monts, had attempted to establish a colony on nearby Dochets Island, which they named Isle Ste. Croix. King Henry IV of France had appointed de Monts his viceroy in Acadia—the area now embracing Nova Scotia and New Brunswick—and had also given him a monopoly of the region's fur trade. De Monts is believed to have settled on the tiny island, less than a mile and one-half in circumference, with few trees and no fresh water, because it would have been easy to defend against an attack by the Indians. During the winter of 1604-05 his party of seventy, consisting of aristocrats, sailors, Swiss mercenaries and transported convicts, were the only white men between Florida and the North Pole. Reduced before spring to a diet of salted meat and melted snow they were attacked by scurvy. Thirty-five of them died. In August 1605 the survivors moved across the Bay of Fundy where they helped to build Port Royal.

The first Europeans known to have settled on Campobello were the family of Jean Sarreau, Sieur de St. Aubin, who was granted the seigniory of Passamaquoddie [sic] in 1684. M. Sarreau surrounded his house with a palisade. A census taken in 1689 listed the inhabitants of the island as four men, four women, eight boys, five girls, four horses and seven horned cattle.

This was the period of the great struggle between France and England for control of North America. Acadia changed hands nine times in the seventeenth and eighteenth centuries. New England and New France were effectively at war even when old England and old France were technically at peace. The conflict was embittered both by the old hatreds engen-

The Port Royal Habitation, site of one of the earliest European settlements in North America.

dered by religion and the new hatreds inspired by nationalism. At intervals the French and their Indian allies swept down from Acadia to raid outlying New England settlements, lay the land waste and kill or enslave the inhabitants. In their turn the English and New Englanders conducted raids into Acadia, burning houses, barns and crops, and butchering cattle. Even the tiny establishment of the Sieur de St. Aubin was not permitted to be neutral and in 1692 the seigneur's son and another man named Jacques Petipas were captured and taken as prisoners to Boston. A census taken in 1693 showed that the settlement had shrunk to three adults and four children. Having obtained permission to return to France, the Sieur de St. Aubin, by now a penniless and broken man of eighty-two, left the island in 1703. He died two years later, on the other side of the Bay of Fundy, at Port Royal. Death came to him there "in the house of an inhabitant who had received him through charity."

Although Port Royal was the capital of Acadia, it contained only seventy or eighty houses and its fort was garrisoned by only about 250 soldiers. The French had no other place of strength in the colony. In 1710 Port Royal was besieged and captured by New England militiamen, the "Bostonnais," who considered it a nest of pirates who preyed on the New England fisheries. They changed its name to Annapolis Royal in honour of their Queen Anne. The fall of Port Royal meant the conquest of Acadia which became Her Britannic Majesty's province of Nova Scotia. The perils of life on the frontier in that turbulent era are rather quaintly illustrated by Hibbert Newton in his account of a visit that he paid to Campobello in 1722. The island was then inhabited by a French family named Dambois. Mr. Newton, collector of customs at Annapolis Royal, was on his way to Boston aboard the sloop *Ipswich* of which James Blinn was owner and master. Of his adventures on the island, he wrote:

> It was Earlely ye 13th wee came to an Anchor att a place called Otter Harbour in passimaquada. As near as I can guess about six a clock, the Boat was hoisted out and Mr. Blinn, Mr. Savage, Mr. Adams Jun'., my son Tommy not quite four Years of Age, with Mr. Savages Negro man and two Sailors belonging to the Sloop, went on shore, with a Design to have refreshed ourselves at Mons Dambois's house the people lookt very Dejected, and Melancholy at our entering their house, but the reason we could not Imagine, till Leaveing the Old man's house, we went a quarter of a mile farther to his sons house, where is the place the Flakes are, that they dry their Fish on, we were all Looking at the Fish, when on a Sudden one Pierre Neptune an Indian, with twelve Other Indians seized on Mr. Blinn with their Axes in their hands, and Naked Knives very near as Long as a Bugginett. Mr. Blinn at the first Struggled with them, then one of the Indians clapt his knife to his side, and had he made the least resistance would in all probability have stabbed him. We demanded the Meaning of this Treatment: and they answered us, it was warr, and we their

prisoners. . . . Mr. Blinn Started up and asked him that Called himself Chief, what they would be att, and what they wanted. They told him his sloop and all his Cargoe, now in the time they were securing us, Two of our Boat Crew slipt into the Boat, and were got half way to the sloop, before the Indians Discovered them. When they did they Order'd Mr. Blinn to hale them a shore, but instead of that, they not understanding our Language, Mr. Blinn called to them to do as he had Ordered them that was to bring the Sloop to Saile which accordingly they did. We were verry much concern'd when we saw the Sloop had left us, and were in great fear the Indians might do us Some Mischiefs, for they were continually wetting their knives and Swinging their hatchets in their hands, however God Almighty's providence so Order'd it they did us no harm but pointed to us to go into the Cannoes, and carried us to Dambois' house when they agreed to release us Mr. Blinn paying them, twenty seven pistoles, wch Dambois did for him in Indian Corn powder shot &c. and with things they had from on board the Sloop, amounted to about 60 pound. Before it was night two of the Dambois's went in a Birch Cannoe to acquaint Mr. Blinn's people to bring the Shallop to us as soon as it was dark which accordingly they did. . . . As soon as it was day rowed the Shallop out of the Harbour, it being quite calm. We had not rowed Long, before we had a hard gale at N.N.W. wch by the blessing of God carried us safe from the hands of the Salvages [sic].

One is inclined to feel that Mr. Newton's "salvages" were extraordinarily lenient with their captives. Despite Mr. Blinn's abortive resistance and continued defiance they did nothing worse than intimidate him into providing them with a fairly modest quantity of such necessities as corn, powder and shot. Their patience becomes more surprising still when one reflects on how their nation had suffered since its invasion by Europeans. In 1760 Michael Neptune, chief of the Passamaquoddies, went to the new capital of Halifax, Nova Scotia, to talk with these English who had succeeded the French as masters of his people. He told them that famine and disease had so afflicted the Passamaquoddies that the number of their fighting men had been reduced from 1,400 to 350. They gave him a blanket and a laced hat.

Chapter two ❦ 1767-1769

No man will be a sailor who has contri-
vance enough to get himself into a jail;
for being in a ship is being in a jail, with
the chance of being drowned.
                                    —Samuel Johnson

Among the thousands of jobless soldiers and sailors who
flocked to London in the early 1760's at the close of England's
triumphant Seven Years' War with France there was a Welsh
naval officer named William Owen, whose appearance was
such that he could have been the model for the Old Salt on a
Toby jug. Lieutenant Owen had a nose like a poniard and the
full, florid face characteristic of the English gentleman in an
era when he might sit down to a dinner of trout, salmon,
soles, veal, ham, boiled fowl, beef, mutton, pie, pudding,
gooseberries, currants and cherries, and afterwards imbibe
two bottles of brandy-primed sherry, port, marsala or

madeira. His gold-braided right sleeve was empty and before long a patch would cover his right eye. The arm he had lost to the Mounseers at the Battle of Pondicherry in 1760, when the subjects of King George III and the subjects of King Louis XIV contended for the riches of India like famished tigers fighting over a great hunk of fresh meat. The eye was destined to be sacrificed in a less ostentatious kind of warfare: pierced by a meat-hook during an election riot. This was an age of which it has been said that, while few Englishmen could vote, any Englishman was free to throw a dead cat at the Prime Minister.

Men such as Lieutenant Owen were in a sour mood. Many of them felt that their government had betrayed them and thrown away the fruits of victory. The Seven Years' War had begun in North America, where it came to be known as the French and Indian War. The French had attempted to cut off the western expansion of British North America at the Allegheny Mountains by establishing a chain of forts linking Quebec and Louisiana. England not only broke the chain but under the brilliant leadership of William Pitt defeated the French in the West Indies, Africa and India, and took possession of the whole of Canada. This being the middle of the eighteenth century, a period refreshingly free of cant, neither Pitt nor his chief backers, the merchant princes of the City of London, saw any need to fabricate a sanctimonious ideology in justification of their war. They freely admitted that the stakes were such staples as tea, sugar, furs and fish. By the time of the signing of the Treaty of Paris that formally ended hostilities, Pitt and his supporters had been replaced in Parliament by an anti-war party led by the Earl of Bute, the royal favourite, and backed by the great landowners who resented the manner in which the war had increased their taxes while it enriched mere vulgar tradesmen. To the disgust of officers such as Lieutenant Owen, England gave the French West In-

Opposite: the Owen Family T with the date of Captain William Owen's death given erroneously as 1788 instead of 1778.

Jenkyn Owen b1620
Owen Owen b1650
Owen Owen b1678
David Owen b1700 d1777

Owen Owen of Tynycoed b1723 d1789

Rev Edward Owen Rector of Warrington b1728 d1805

Capt William Owen Royal Navy Granted Campobello 1767
(by Lord William Campbell Governor of Nova Scotia)
b1735 d1788

Sir Arthur Owen Kt of Glansevern, Mont Wales b1752 d1816

William Owen of Glansevern b1752 d1829

Mary Owen m Thomas Jones

David Owen of Campobello (1789-1829) b1754 d1829

Adml Sir E W C R Owen GCB GCH b(at Campobello) 1772 d1847 Of Windlesham House Buried at Windlesham

Adml W Fitzwilliam Owen b1774 d1857 Of Campobello Buried at Campobello

Edward Jones (Johnes) b1770 d1841 m. Mary Davis

Portia Owen b1819 d1865 m.1847 Clement Hemery Esqr of Mont Plaisir Jersey C.I. no issue.

Cornelia Owen b1820 d1896 m.1839 Capt H S Robinson Royal Navy of Campobello (Island sold 1879) & Wallisham House Surrey

Eliza Johnes m. Erskine Humphreys b1807 d1877

Owen Campobello Robinson-Owen b1840 d1914 Lt Devon Regt

Portia b1842 d1889 sisters Mary

John Hemery Robinson-Owen b1845 d1890 Lt Royl Ny

Cornelia Ramsay b1847 d1925 m.1873 Gustavus B E Cochrane Royl Ny of Wallisham House Surrey

Everyl Rose b1885 d1896

A C Humphreys-Owen of Glansevern Mont Wales b1836 d1905

Captain Archibald Cochrane Engr Royal Navy b1874 Of Wallisham House Surrey m.1904 Maye only daughter of A dal V Brooke RE

Grizel Martha Lily Owen Cochrane Royl Ny b1876

Captain Edward Owen Cochrane Royl Ny b1881 m.1908 Molly only daughter of Col Fitz George C B

Everyl Rose b1885 d1896

A E Humphreys-Owen b1876

Stephen Humphreys-Owen b1907

Marie Cecila Grizel Rosemary Morwa Frances Mary Stella Dorothea

James Owen Cochrane b1914

Suzanne Flora

dies and the fishing rights off Newfoundland back to France and, still worse, returned Cuba and the Philippines to France's ally, Spain.

But Lieutenant Owen was chiefly preoccupied with his own problems. Now a man in his thirties he had followed the sea since he was a child. This was the century in which twelve-year-old midshipmen played leapfrog on the decks of men-o'-war while awaiting the signal to go into action against the enemy. Now he was a sailor without a ship. Moreover, like many naval officers and unlike most army officers of the day, he had limited funds. His family was old and respectable, but its estate in Wales was a modest one. There survives a watercolour sketch of the Owen's modest, comfortable-looking house at Glensevern; it is evocative of the farm rather than of the manor. His brother was High Sheriff of Montgomeryshire; but Lieutenant Owen was a fourth son in a time and place when fourth sons of the gentry were expected to live by their wits and their elders' generosity. So he had entreated the Lords of the Admiralty for some "gratuity, pension or preferment," pointing out that besides losing an arm in attempting to cut out two French ships from under the guns of Pondicherry he had been wounded by a musket ball that had lodged in his body for above three and one-half years, and that his long service in the "un-Christian" climate of the East Indies had greatly impaired his health.

No doubt he followed through with a good deal of lobbying, haunting the anterooms and drawing rooms of the great and imploring various influential lords and ladies to exert themselves on his behalf, in the style described by James Boswell in his *London Journal*. And doubtlessly the one-armed Welsh sailor, like the young Scots adventurer, visited taverns and coffee houses, ate beefsteaks at chop houses, bet on cock fights, went to see David Garrick play at Drury Lane, and watched "Jack Ketch" officiate at the hanging of highwaymen and pickpockets. We know from the Lieutenant's diary that one night he threatened to use his sword to cut off the noses and ears of some catchpolls who were attempting to arrest one of his friends and to imprison him for his wife's debts.

Their Lordships of the Admiralty ignored the Lieutenant's petition, but he had better luck with a letter to his old commander, Lord William Campbell, with whom he had served five years in India. Lord William had recently been appointed Governor of Nova Scotia through the influence of his father, the Duke of Argyll.

Lieutenant Owen wrote:

> I arrived in London about four months ago. After long attendance and great solicitations, I am at length put off with a pitiful Pension, with which I am going to retire into the Country among my relations for the remainder of my days unless something unexpected happens to enable me to obtain the promotion I think I have a right to. . . . I have spent a great deal of money in Town, have no Fortune, and want a sum soon on a very urgent Occasion. . . . I hope, notwithstanding the disparity between us in point of Rank and Fortune, that your Lordship will honour me with a continuance of the Friendship and Regard, which I had reason to imagine existed between us during the Five years we Messed together."

To which Lord William, whom an historian has described as "a popular young hero, a man of few ideas, ingenuous but relatively honest and generous," wrote this reply:

> London, July 8th, 1766. My dear Owen. I shall go abroad in a public Character and to a very healthy part of the World not a great way off. If you chuse to go with me I shall make it a point for you first to get the rank of a Master and Commander, and shall have it in my power, I fancy, to do something for you there. I am in good health, as is Lady William and the little one.

I can give you no more lights as yet, as it is a secret. Let me hear from you by the return of Post. I am in a very great hurry. I beg you will excuse this scrawl and remain, Yours to Command, W. Campbell.

Halifax, Nova Scotia, in 1764: the early Campobello settlers' first view of North America.

Lieutenant Owen was promoted to captain and engaged as secretary to the newly appointed Governor. In the fall of 1766 he accompanied his patron to Nova Scotia. After spending the winter in Halifax, he devoted the summer of 1767 to surveying and mapping the province's Shubenacadie Lakes. On September 30 of that year, Lord William, acting in his capacity as "Governor-in-Chief, Captain-General and Vice-Admiral of Nova Scotia and its dependencies," named Captain Owen Principal Proprietary of the Great Outer Island of Passamaquoddy. He had kept his promise to "do something" for his friend. Furthermore he had arranged matters so that the Captain received a much larger grant than that to which his rank entitled him—first, by describing the island as containing

Sunset over North Lubec from Friar Bay beach, with Friar Head at left

One of Campobello's welcoming beaches

One of the luxuriant forest scenes found in Roosevelt Campobe International Park

only four thousand acres when actually it was three times that size and, second, since even that was more acreage than the law allowed, by including the Captain's three young nephews as joint grantees.

Captain Owen was surprisingly dilatory in taking possession of his domain. In the fall of 1767 he sailed back to England—after touring New England but without visiting his island. The following year he travelled in France and the Netherlands, and became involved in the political brawl that cost him his eye. Perhaps he was not eager to remove himself to so remote a corner of the world. Maybe he hoped that something better would turn up—ideally a pension that would permit him to live like a gentleman or, if not that, then the captaincy of one of His Majesty's ships of the line. India— now there was a country where a gentleman of bottom with a bit of luck and the right connections could make enough money in three years to enable him to live like a Duke for the rest of his life! But what did British America have to offer aside from codfish and beaver skins? Voltaire had dismissed Canada contemptuously as a "few acres of snow."

It was not until August 28, 1769, that Captain Owen and a group of his friends assembled to discuss plans for the settlement and development of his grant. They met at a coffee house in Warrington, about midway between Liverpool and Manchester, where the Captain's brother was rector. Daniel Defoe describes Warrington as "a large, populous old built town, but rich and full of good country tradesmen," adding that it was the site of a weekly market for linen, and that the linen sold at this market was "generally speaking a sort of table linen, called huk-a-back or huk-a-buk; 'tis well known among the good housewives, so I need not describe it." Now, here in the north of England, the shape of things to come was already beginning to unfold. Liverpool, with its population of

100,000 was the second or third largest town in the kingdom, a great port whose wealth had been based originally on the slave trade, and now a commercial centre where goods from the ends of the earth were stored in warehouses eight or nine storeys tall. Manchester was the birthplace of the Industrial Revolution, then entering its squalid infancy; the Captain and his friends were young enough to live to see the time when it became a metropolis where some accumulated vast fortunes, while others lived ten to a room, without furniture or even beds, and were thrown into pits called Poor Holes when they died. Warrington, then, was an appropriate place for a meeting of would-be empire-builders.

The old agricultural England of small independent yeoman farmers was beginning to give way to the new industrial England of owners and labourers. The process was already under way that would leave some few of the yeomen's children on the land as servants of the squires and nobles while the rest were driven into the towns, where they became factory hands, some of whom worked eighteen hours a day, every day of the year except Sundays, Good Friday and Christmas. A year earlier James Watt had patented the steam engine that would make it possible for the factories to employ thousands as compared to the few score employed when their source of power had been water. A canal was being dug between Manchester and Liverpool and would be opened in 1773, one of the many waterways that would greatly speed up an inland transportation system that until then had depended on roads that not infrequently were eighteen inches deep in mud. For the middle and upper classes these were boom times. Men who possessed capital were in a speculative mood.

It is not difficult to picture the Captain and his associates gathered about a table in their blue frock coats, brass buttons, lace cravats, red or yellow waistcoats, breeches and riding boots. No doubt they smoked clay pipes and drank brandy or port as they talked, capping their discussions with a supper, perhaps of cold beef, rabbit and the local Cheshire cheese, their nightcaps consisting of a gill of gin with a bit of sugar in it.

The times were ripe for ventures such as theirs.

Here is the Captain's own account of the outcome of that meeting:

The 28th in the evening, there was a meeting of my friends held at the Coffee House to consider about a plan of settling, cultivating and improving the outer or great island of Passamaquoddy, situated in the Bay of Fundy, Nova Scotia, wch had been granted me when in North-America. The following scheme was proposed, which I closed with, and proper instructions were given to our Attorney to draw up the necessary writings; after previously signing the articles or heads thereof. Suppose the whole property to consist of sixteen parts or shares; thirteen of them were to be at all expenses in carrying out the plan, and I as lord of the soil or principal proprietary to be at no expense whatever, and to have 3/16th of the net produce. The shares to be transferable if the parties were approved of by a majority of the proprietors, and any person growing tired of the plan, refusing or neglecting to pay into the hands of the treasurer or chief manager, when properly demanded, his quota for carrying on the undertaking, to forfeit his share in the island, as well as in the fund for its trade, settlement, cultivation or improvement. A Vessel was agreed to be bought. I was solicited to take possession of the island, and many other material points were discussed and finally settled. The subscribing Proprietors were Roger Rogerson of Warrington, Esqr., two shares; Mr. Hodson of Wegan, two do; John Lyons, Esqr., Edd Pemberton, M.D., Rev. Edward Owen, A.M., and William Turner, Esqr., all of Warrington, one share each, Messrs. Lloyd and Kerfoot of do and do; Thomas Hayward of the Royal Navy, one share; Messrs. Samuel Johnson and Rowland Hunter, Merchants of Liverpool, and Plato Denny, Mariner and Ship-master of do, three shares; making in all thirteen shares, or 13/16 of the whole.

Now it was up to the Captain to find settlers and a ship.

A brig. The Snow Owen *that landed at Campobello in 1770 possessed a third mast rigged with fore and aft sails that could be used in place of the others in rough weather.*

Chapter three 🌿 1770-1772

> He that is rich and wants to fool away
> A sporting sum in North Americay,
> Let him subscribe himself a headlong sharer
> And asses' ears will honour him, or bearer.
> — 18th-century English ballad

The ship that Captain Owen bought in February 1770 was a snow: similar to a brig except that in addition to two square-rigged masts it possessed a try-mast rigged with a fore and aft sail that could be used in place of the other sails in rough weather. Not very imaginatively, the Captain christened her the *Snow Owen*.

In March the following advertisement appeared in the Liverpool *General Advertiser:*

> *For Halifax and the Island of*
> *Passamaquoddy, in Nova Scotia,*
> *The SNOW OWEN, Plato Denny, Master.*
> *Burthen, 180 tons, will sail about*
> *27th inst. March.*
> *For freight or passage apply to*
> *the said Master on board the vessel*
> *in the South Dock; to Mr. Roger*
> *Rogerson, in Warrington, and to*
> *Mr. Rowland Hunter, Liverpool.*

Captain Owen acquired thirty-eight Lancashire settlers, a few of them former seamen but most of them indentured servants. Since poor persons could not afford the cost of their passage to America (ten or twelve pounds, which was as much as some of them earned in a year), the only feasible way for many of them to reach the New World was by signing an indenture, contracting themselves into semi-slavery with a planter or shipowner. Such servitude lasted for four or five, and in some cases for seven or more, years. The master could work such servants as long and as hard as he liked and give them such food, clothing and shelter as he chose. They could not marry without his consent, and if they ran away and were caught they could be punished by having a year or more added to their term of service. Their hope lay in the promise that when their indentures expired they would be given grants of land and become free men. Indentured servants were recruited from the class that men of the Captain's rank in society called the lower orders, the rabble or the swinish multitude.

The Captain had to go on board sooner than he had expected because his passengers, as he recorded tersely in his diary, had become "riotous and disorderly." Many of them had been separated from their wives or husbands. It is unlikely that many of them had ever before been as far as fifty miles from their birthplace. Now they were to be shipped across three thousand miles of ocean to a wilderness from which they might never return. The gin shops advertised "Drunk for a penny, dead drunk for tuppence, clean straw for nothing." For these colonists the only alternative to servitude abroad was starvation at home. No doubt they had used what pennies they had to buy temporary forgetfulness.

They lived close enough to the sea to be accustomed to the tall masts, the great folds of sail, the groaning webs of rigging, the pointing bowsprit. But at such times as they could muster the stomach to come on deck they must have been overwhelmed by the sight of the open and seemingly limitless ocean. One supposes that for most of the voyage they kept to their narrow and foul-smelling quarters below decks where rats prowled in the stifling heat and the only ventilation came through hatches that were battened down in foul weather. Their diet probably consisted of salt beef, ship's biscuit and water to which it was necessary to add more and more vinegar. The *Snow Owen* encountered "hail, sleet and rain — a high, cross and confused sea." The vessel began to leak. Eight days out the Captain noted wryly that his landsmen were "seasick and sick of the sea."

They anchored at Halifax, Nova Scotia, on May 21, 1770, after a voyage of forty-five days. Captain Owen confided proudly to his diary that he was met as soon as he landed "by many of the principal inhabitants." These were bad years for the town that had been founded in 1749 to counter-balance the great French fortress at Louisbourg on Cape Breton Island.

Halifax had lost its military and naval importance with the fall of Louisbourg in 1758 and of Quebec in 1759. Its subsidy from England had been lowered from 50,000 pounds sterling to one-tenth of that amount, and its population which a few years earlier had reached 6,000 was now down to less than 2,000. Still, in the week that they spent there the Lancashire settlers probably decided that the New World was not quite so alien as they had anticipated. Men in King George's uniform walked the streets, although many of the troops normally stationed in Halifax had been shipped off to Boston, where unrest was so great that the British had called in all the soldiers they could muster. The town's proudest edifice, St. Paul's, was a thoroughly English church, although of wood rather than of stone. Nova Scotia was now in the hands of the New England planters who had arrived during the previous fifteen years to take up the plowlands, pastures, gardens and orchards from which New England militiamen had driven the Acadians in 1755.

Before leaving Halifax, Captain Owen had himself appointed magistrate for Sunbury County, to "Make me formidable and respected in my island and neighbourhood," he explained. Sunbury County was then the name of what became New Brunswick following the American War of Independence. At the same time, Captain Plato Denny was appointed a justice of the peace, as was Captain Owen's clerk, William Isherwood.

At five o'clock on June 3, 1770, six days out from Halifax and with a fresh breeze from the west, the *Snow Owen* "carried out the kedge anchor and moored in the northeast cove of Harbour de L'Outre in the Island of Passamaquoddy."

There was a streak of whimsy in that stout old sea dog, William Owen. Certainly there was a bit of Welsh drollery in his choice of a name for his island. He was practically duty-

St. Paul's Anglican Church in 1764, colonial Halifax's proudest edifice.

bound to name it for his patron. But instead of calling it simply Lord William's Island or Campbell Island or even, a little more fancifully, New Argyll, he chose to call it Campo Bello, "partly complimentary and punning on the name of the governor," he said, and partly as applicable to the island's beauty and fertility — "*Campo bello* being, so I presume, the Spanish and Italian equivalent of the French *beauchamp* or the English *fair field*." (Although the name *Campo Bello* was used until late in the nineteenth century, the modern *Campobello* has been employed, for the sake of simplicity, throughout this book.) Then, as though his inventiveness were exhausted, he decided that the town he intended to build would be called *New Warrington*, and his harbour, *Port Owen*.

The Captain soon learned that his Lancashire settlers were not Campobello's only inhabitants. Three families of New Englanders had already established themselves there, including a stubborn and canny Scotch-Irishman named Robert Wilson, who had come to the island in 1765, and his strong-willed and fiery-tempered wife, Mary. While the Captain was quick to point out to them that they had no legal right to be there, he seems to have been pleased rather than disturbed by their presence — especially after he had seen them at work, devoting their hard-earned frontier ingenuity and initiative to helping provide shelter and a source of food for his Johnny Raw Lancashiremen. The New Englanders, so the Captain decided, possessed "superior abilities" when it came to coping with the wilderness. Each of them was carpenter, farmer, fisherman and seaman. They were healthy, robust and industrious, and their lasses were fair, handsome and good-natured. They pleased him so well that he agreed not to charge them rent, whereupon, as he later recorded, they "cheerfully acquiesced" in coming under his jurisdiction. Before long he was to advertise in Boston in hope of attracting more New England settlers.

*A 1777 view of Campobello,
showing Captain Owen's
settlement of New Warrington.*

Future relations between the Owen and Wilson families were to be far less harmonious.

The Lancashiremen, the New Englanders and the fifteen-man crew of the *Snow Owen* worked together with a will. Two large buildings were hastily erected, one temporarily to house the settlers and the other to provide shelter for their provisions. While some of the settlers planted potatoes, turnips and grain, others fished for cod, haddock and pollock. The Captain's diary provides some glimpses into life as it went on during those first months in the history of his settlement:

> June 10, 1770 — Sunday the tenth, having no better place yet, I performed Divine Service in the Shed, both morning and evening, at which attended most of the inhabitants of the Indian and Casco Bay Islands.
>
> The 16th erected a flagstaff 44 feet high on the summit of the hill near the centre of the intended town. — William Clark of this island swore an assault, battery and breach of the peace against William Dollard of Deer Island; granted a warrant and sent a Party to apprehend him, who seized and brought him over handcuffed about midnight.
>
> The 21st went over in the Yawl to Point Pleasant, and Married Philip Newton and Mary Cartney, widow, James Boyd Esqr. a justice of the peace appearing personally and giving a certificate of his having published their bans three Sundays in time to Divine worship, agreeable to act of the Province Assembly.
>
> Sunday, the 1st July, performed Divine Service morning and evening and baptized a son of William and Susanna Clark.
>
> The 13th sent two new salmon nets up to Scoodic falls by James Cochran to fish upon shares; whilst our own fishermen are daily employed in the Cod, Haddock and Pollock fishery.
>
> Sunday, the 22nd I was visited by M. Baille the French missionary and about thirty of the principle [sic] Indians of the Passamaquoddy and St. John's tribes. Divine service and preached a sermon.

The 3rd [August] a pair of stocks and wipping post was erected near what we called the Market-gate, to deter and punish the unruly, disorderly and dishonest.

The reaction of the Indians to Captain Owen's sermon must have been polite, for he was sufficiently pleased that he bought from them a 444-pound moose and had it barbecued and served to his people. The Captain liked to seal his agreements with the Indians with a drink of killibogus, a mixture of rum and spruce beer. This was an age when "a drink" normally meant a quarter of a pint. Rum was generally known as "kill-devil", and the recipe for spruce beer was as follows:

> Take seven pounds of good spruce and boil it well till the bark peels off. Then take the spruce out and put in three gallons of molasses and boil the liquor again, scum it well as it boils, then take it out of the kettle and put it in a cooler. When milk-warm in the cooler put a pint of yeast into it and mix well. Then put in the barrel and let it work for two or three days, and keep filling it up as it works out. When done working, bung it up with a tent-peg in the barrel to give it vent now and then. It may be used in two or three days.

Spruce beer is still made and drunk in some parts of the Maritime Provinces, notably in New Brunswick's Miramichi country, although not—as far as is known—on Campobello.

If the "wipping post" was ever used there is no record of it, but the Captain reports that he punished a man for stealing rum by putting him in the stocks with a sign on his back reading, "A thief, a liar, and a drunkard." One wonders if, after inflicting that punishment, the Captain went home and relaxed with a gill of killibogus.

A report prepared in the summer of 1770 showed that the settlers had planted wheat, oats, barley, rye, peas, clover, hemp, flax, potatoes, turnips, apple trees and plum trees. They had cleared and fenced land for hay. Fifteen houses had been built and it was planned to build a grist mill and a chapel to be called George Chapel in honour of the King whose thirty-first birthday it had been on that day the previous year when the Principal Proprietary first set eyes on his island. There were twenty-nine head of cattle; trade had started: the settlement had sent 110 tons of lumber to England and was engaged to send 700 tons more; potash had also been shipped to the English market, and shingles and cord wood had been exported to Boston. Rum and sugar from the West Indies were landed at Campobello and reshipped to Saint John where they were traded for beaver skins.

The highest paid man among the Captain's retainers was the clerk, William Isherwood, whose pay had been raised from £60 to £100 that year. Many of the male servants were paid only six shillings a week, and some of the women, listed as "cooks, housewives, washerwomen and spruce beer brewers," received a weekly stipend of only one shilling and sixpence.

The population now consisted of seventy-three persons, thirty-six of them English and thirty-seven of them New Englanders. But here, there lay a problem that boded ill for the future of the English colony, for while almost all the New Englanders lived with their families, there were only four married couples among the English. Moreover, men outnumbered women by more than two to one, the total population consisting of fifty-one males and twenty-two females. Many of these men, longing for the wives and children they had left behind them in Liverpool or Manchester, must have felt that their island home was little better than a prison.

In 1771, Captain Owen became a father. It is believed that the mother of the future Admiral Sir Edward William Campbell Rich Owen was the Captain's housekeeper, Sarah Haslem. The Captain liked to refer to the child as "the Hereditary

Captain William Owen, the first Principal Proprietary of the Great Outer Island of Passamaquoddy, which he christened "Campo Bello."

Prince of Campobello." Certainly the Principal Proprietary must have felt like a sovereign prince that year when he received an official visit from Governor Lord William Campbell who arrived on the sloop *Senegal*, under the command of Sir Thomas Rich, baronet, accompanied by a schooner and an eighteen-ton cutter. The *Senegal* paid its respects to the Principal Proprietary with a salute of thirteen guns before Lord William and his officers came on shore, where a guard of honour was drawn up to welcome them with three volleys of musketry. Upon his guests' departure several weeks later, Captain Owen was able to treat them in even grander style, for in the interim he had bought Captain Rich's cutter for fifty-two guineas, christened her the *Campobello Packet*, and mounted her with coehorn and swivel guns. When the *Senegal* fired a farewell eleven-gun salute, the gunners of the *Campobello Packet* echoed her.

Among those who witnessed the various salutes was a party of Indians from the mainland who had been presented with a Union Jack and had promised to give up their French military commissions. No doubt the thunder of the guns was intended to impress them with the awesome power of His Britannic Majesty.

One purpose of the Governor's visit was to study the disputed boundary between the colonies of Nova Scotia and Massachusetts (what would now be the border between New Brunswick and Maine). In Champlain's time the boundary had been set at the St. Croix River. But there were three rivers in the area and by this time nobody, not even the Indians whom Lord William questioned about it, knew for certain which of them had originally been named the St. Croix. (Eventually, in 1797 relics of Champlain's domicile on Dochets Island established the Scoodic as the "true St. Croix.") While the Governor's visit shed little light on the matter of the boundary, it did provide the opportunity for Lord William and Sir Thomas to become godfathers to Captain Owen's son.

In the fall of 1771 Captain Owen set out in the *Campobello Packet* to fetch supplies for the winter. But on his way to Boston he met a ship bringing the necessary provisions and so his voyage turned into a holiday. What the Captain described as an "odd adventure" took place when the *Campobello Packet's* New England pilot, Aaron Bunker, paid a surprise visit to his home on Cranberry Island off the Maine coast.

Here is how the Captain tells it:

Alas! the dire mishap! he popped in very unexpectedly I suppose, and found his maiden sister Mary bundled abed with the son of rather a wealthy settler on Deer Island. The enraged pilot swore he would cut the gallant's throat, if he did not repair the honour of the family by marrying his sister; the trembling swain declared his readiness to do so as soon as he had an opportunity, but observed there was no parson in the district, nor any Justice of the Peace nearer than Frenchman's Bay. "Leave that to me," says Aaron; off he came to me this morning & explained the whole affair; soliciting me in the most earnest terms to do the good office for the family. I told him that the affair could not be done with propriety without a formal licence or due publication of banns, and moreover that I was out of my district. But as the last point was not quite clear, the western boundary of Sunbury never having been determined, I would strain it to remove a blot out of the escutcheon of the Bunker family. The skipper of the *Dolphin* schooner had been married at Indian Island a few days before we sailed by James Boyd Esqr., but neither himself or his bride being perfectly satisfied with his mode of linking them together, they requested the favour of me to do that good office for them likewise. In short, I went ashore about eleven o'clock, and was escorted by a numerous party to Isaac Bunker's house, where I married Eliachim Eaton to Mary Bunker; and remarried Robert

M'lellan to Jerusha Frost. A good substantial and plentiful entertainment was provided on the occasion, and a real and genuone [sic] Yankee frolic ensued.

The Captain had a distinctly eighteenth-century sense of "frolic." He derived great sport, for instance, from what he called "driving." That is driving sea fowl into the bed of the creek at what is now St. Andrews, New Brunswick, where men, women and children used paddles and bludgeons to kill hundreds of ducks, murrs and coots.

William Owen enjoyed being Prince of Campobello. But he was first of all an officer of the Royal Navy. On June 14, 1771, he had received word that war with France was imminent. In his diary he wrote that "such a report had for some time prevailed among the Indians who bye the bye, in their hearts still bore a stronger affection and warmer attachment towards their old friends the French than the English." It was inevitable that he would once again try his luck on the quarterdeck. His brother, the rector of Warrington, had written to Sir Edward Hawke, Lord of the Admiralty, informing him of Captain Owen's "absence abroad and reminding him of former promises." But as Captain Owen recorded, "tho my brother was at least as well born and bred, infinitely better educated, stood highly exalted as a man, and not obscure or undignified in the Church, this mighty Chief never deigned to answer his letter.... But let me not enter into revengeful or malignant invective against this bloated whale." On the rector's advice the Captain determined to return to England in hope of obtaining an appointment from Sir Edward Hawke's successor, the Earl of Sandwich.

When he set sail for England, Captain Owen was accompanied by his son, whom he later left in the care of Sir Thomas Rich, so that the boy might be reared as an English gentleman while the father was away to the wars. No doubt

Prince Cottage,
Roosevelt Campobello
International Park

*Fishing is the island's
chief means of livelihood.*

the child's mother, the servant Sarah Haslem, had mixed emotions: she had lost her son, but she could be sure that he would grow up as a member of his father's social class. Her own status in later years seems to have been little better than that of a camp follower despite the fact that in Manchester, on September 17, 1774, she bore the Captain a second son, the future Admiral William Fitzwilliam Owen.

Captain Owen wrote of his departure from Campobello:

> . . . in the morning I embarked my family, servants and baggage and soon after went on board myself, accompanied by all the principal people of the District. About noon weighed and towed out of the harbour, attended by the *Campobello Packet,* and was soon after saluted with seven guns and three cheers from Flaggstaff-hill. To which I returned five guns and three cheers. As soon as out of the harbour, a fresh breeze sprung up from the Southward, with which we stood down the Sound; and at three o'clock, being about 3 miles to the westward of the Wolves [two small islands between Campobello and Grand Manan; Champlain had called them the "Magpies"], the Gentlemen of Campobello having washed down their dinners, brought to, sent them on board the Cutter, and she stood in for the Island again; the gale now freshened at SW and WSW, as soon as the Yawl returned, hoisted her in, took the 1st reefs in the topsails and made sail.

With Captain Owen gone, Captain Plato Denny was authorized to "direct, conduct and superintend" the affairs of the island. But the period of servitude for many of the indentured servants was about to expire, and they had never ceased to dream of their real home on the other side of the Atlantic. A few months after Captain Owen's departure, twenty-seven of them persuaded Captain Denny to take them back to Lancashire. Was he a man with a degree of compassion rare in his century? Or had the settlers, and perhaps the sailors as well, threatened to mutiny if their exile was not ended? Perhaps he himself was homesick. We do not know. We only know that late in 1772 the *Snow Owen* sailed for Liverpool.

She never reached her destination.

The *Snow Owen*, the captain with the intriguing name, her crew and all her passengers were lost at sea.

Chapter four ❦ *1772-1786*

The world's turned upside down.

— *Title of a song popular during the*
American War of Independence

When the *Snow Owen* sank beneath the Atlantic, only nine of
the original Lancashire settlers remained on Campobello.
Soon seven of them drifted away to the mainland, leaving
only Andrew Lloyd, formerly an apprentice to Captain
Denny, and his wife, Mary Lawless, whose father, a gardener
who served as the islanders' barber, had fought as a sergeant
under Wolfe at Quebec. Andrew Lloyd was to become the
only Campobello man known to have enlisted in the American War of Independence, serving with the Royal American
Fencibles. Obviously he was a man with a mind of his own —
as was his grandson, William Lloyd Garrison, who became

the fire-eating editor of the abolitionist journal *The Liberator*, who thundered that if the United States constitution did not prohibit slavery then it, the constitution, ought to be destroyed.

Aside from the Lloyds and the two agents of the Campobello Company, John Moreau and Benjamin Yoxhall, who had been appointed magistrates when Captain Denny left with the *Snow Owen*, the entire population of Campobello now consisted of New Englanders. The scene was set for the conflict between those who owned the land and those who worked it that was to be the central fact of life on the island for the next half-century, and more.

That energetic and astute Scotch-Irishman Robert Wilson had organized a lumber company. Captain Owen, so Wilson told Moreau and Yoxhall, had hired him to cut timber, of which 1,000 tons were still in the woods. He had not been paid, he said, and now he wanted the money that was due to him. Furthermore, Captain Owen had promised to give him legal title to the land that he occupied. What were Moreau and Yoxhall going to do about it? Moreau threw up his hands and left the island, while Yoxhall, who seems to have been made of sterner stuff, refused to present Wilson's bill to the company, that group of investors who had assembled with such high hopes only a few years earlier in an English coffee house.

Wilson either had influential friends in England or, what is more likely, the investors concluded that they were not in a position to beat him and so had better join him. In 1775 they recalled Yoxhall and appointed Wilson in his place. Back in England Yoxhall sourly proclaimed that Wilson was a damn Yankee rebel who had had the effrontery to hoist the American colours on the English flag-staff at Windmill Point. Wilson replied sardonically that he had done so only because he had expected the rebels to seize the island and wanted them to think that he was on their side so that he would be in a better position to protect the company's interests.

These were troubled times. For a while it seemed that Nova Scotia, of which Campobello was still a part, might become the fourteenth colony to rise against King George. Campobello was briefly a refuge for the followers of the Nova Scotian rebel leader, John Allan, whom the Continental Congress at Philadelphia, which co-ordinated the Thirteen Colonies' war efforts, had commissioned superintendent of the eastern Indians and a colonel of infantry. Despite such impressive credentials, Allan was unsuccessful in enlisting the support of either the colonists or the Indians. One chief declared that he was "half-English and half-Boston and would not lift up the hatchet." Allan escaped to the United States at about the same time as his fellow rebel, Colonel Jonathan Eddy, led a futile attack on Fort Cumberland, near what is now Sackville, New Brunswick, at the head of the Bay of Fundy. Meanwhile privateers from both sides sailed in and out of the bay. Congressional troops were encamped at Machias, Maine, and there was a battle at Castine, Maine, not far from Campobello, in which Paul Revere, later celebrated in a poem by Longfellow, fought on the American side and Sir John Moore, destined to become one of England's national heroes, fought for the royalists.

Man O' War Head on Campobello is named for the British sailors stationed near there during the War of Independence. The young officers are said to have planted a garden in which they grew dahlias and marigolds to present to the island girls who "in return for such courtesies consented to dance in winter on the ships' decks regardless of their frozen ear tips." One wintery day two midshipmen accepted a dare to walk around the icy cliffs. Probably they were trying to impress the girls and more than likely they were drunk. What began as a prank ended in disaster when they slipped and plunged to their deaths. Kate Gannett Wells in her nineteenth-century book on Campobello says that "their comrades buried them under the gay flowers"—a neat trick to perform in New Brunswick in the winter!

The Principal Proprietary had departed. Practically all his settlers were gone. Many of the remaining inhabitants were either sympathetic to the rebels or indifferent to the war. Not surprisingly, the Campobello Company decided to throw in its cards. The investors, who had put £16,000 into the project, voted in 1775 to dissolve. Captain Owen and his heirs could have sole possession of Campobello—and much good it was likely to do them.

Unaware of the dissolution of the company and of Captain Owen's death in Madras in 1778, but determined that he was going to be paid, Robert Wilson went to court. The judgment awarded him 2,500 acres of woodland on which lay the disputed timber, together with seventy acres of cleared land containing houses, stores and a windmill. The opening guns had been fired in a land feud that was to last for generations.

Robert Wilson did not live to participate further in that feud. He drowned in 1782, leaving as heirs his sons, Robert, fourteen, and James, eleven. A neighbour, John Curry, who was a shipowner, lumber merchant and justice of the peace, was named as executor. In 1783 the lands were sold by the high sheriff at public auction in Halifax. The buyer was Charles Morris, a Halifax crown surveyor and land speculator. He paid the widow Wilson £500.

In the Treaty of Paris that ended the War of Independence in 1783, the United States pledged itself to protect from persecution, and to restore the estates and property of, those Americans who had sided with the King. The pledge proved impossible to keep. Some of the Loyalists were lynched, many

United Empire Loyalists landing at the site of the present city of Saint John, New Brunswick, in 1783.

were tarred and feathered, others were stoned or found their livestock poisoned—all were ostracized. In the end, 100,000 of them were driven from their homes. A few went to England, a few to the West Indies, but most migrated to what is now Canada, including between 35,000 and 40,000 who settled in what was then Nova Scotia. Almost overnight, Saint John, which previously had been merely a trading-post, was transformed into a town of 5,000, one-third the size of Boston. In 1784, Sunbury County, Nova Scotia (including the island of Campobello), became the new province of New Brunswick, named as if in defiance of the rebels for the German state that was the ancestral seat of King George III. The founders of New Brunswick announced that their intention was to create "the most gentleman-like province on earth." Its capital city (established inland so as to be safe from Yankee privateers in any future war) was named Fredericton in tribute to that Frederick, Duke of York, son of King George III, of whom some wag had written:

> The grand old Duke of York
>   He had 10,000 men.
> He marched them up the hill
>   And then he marched them down again.
>
> And when he was up, he was up.
>   And when he was down, he was down.
> And when he was only halfway up
>   He was neither up nor down.

Nothing had been heard of the Owen family for ten years. It was rumoured and generally believed that the original grant making Captain Owen Principal Proprietary of the island had been revoked. In the summer of 1784, Gilliam Butler, formerly of Boston, bought from Charles Morris the section of the island that Morris had purchased at the sheriff's sale the previous year. The price was £1,111, 2 shillings and 3 pence. Butler, a wheeler-dealer long before the term was invented, was not prepared to pay cash however, and later was to admit that he expected to make so much money out of using Campobello as a base for trade with the United States that he "could give up the property without inconvenience," and presumably without paying the full price for it. Morris took part payment and accepted the rest on credit, but he must have been reassured by the knowledge that Butler had excellent connections. His wife Rebecca was first cousin to Sir John Wentworth, Surveyor General of the King's woods and the last royal Governor of New Hampshire. Soon, Sir John was to be Governor of Nova Scotia, having obtained the post through the influence of his wife, Lady Frances, an intimate friend of the Duke of Clarence, later King William IV.

Butler bought a ship in England, the *Valiant*, and sailed for the Bay of Fundy. With him were his two associates: Captain Thomas Storrow, a former English army officer who had invested most of his dwindling fortune in the adventure, and whose wife, Nancy, was Rebecca Butler's niece; and Storrow's clerk, John Fraser. Butler and Storrow were accompanied by their wives and families. Probably because Storrow did not wish his name, that of a gentleman, publicly associated with trade, the firm was called John Fraser and Company. The Storrows, according to a family historian, went "flattering themselves that the [Passamaquoddy] country would prove an El do Rado."

Leaving the Storrows and Fraser at the mainland town of St. Andrews, then an important lumber port, where they were to represent the company's interests, Butler sailed on to Campobello. Nancy Storrow was later to confess ruefully that her husband had "very little knowledge of business and still less disposition for it."

On Campobello, Butler laid out plans for a settlement to be called Charlottetown, after King George III's queen. He ran a saw mill and a grist mill, traded with the Americans, and sold land to both Yankees and Tories.

Among the Loyalists who came to settle on Campobello, either as squatters or on lots bought from Butler, were officers and men of the Loyal American Regiment, DeLancey's Second Brigade, the Prince of Wales Volunteers and the King's American Legion. Benedict Arnold, the most brilliant of the revolutionary generals before he turned his coat and went over to fight for the King, visited Campobello occasionally on business. In the years immediately following the war, Arnold lived in Saint John, New Brunswick, where he tried to set himself up as a merchant. His efforts failed and, as a former rebel, he was scarcely more popular among his Loyalist neighbours than in the United States where his name had become and was to remain a synonym for traitor. Eventually he sailed away to England, where he died.

Butler was soon involved in a boundary dispute with that formidable lady, the widow Wilson, who claimed that some of the land to which he had taken possession rightfully belonged to her sons, now aged fourteen and seventeen. Worse troubles were to come. He and his partners rapidly discovered that the import-export business was not the easy road to riches that they had imagined. Before long Butler was performing the financial equivalent of doing a juggling act while walking a tightrope. While still in debt to Charles Morris for £800, he was forced to mortgage his share of the island to Captain John McGill of St. Andrews.

An unsuccessful candidate for the New Brunswick Legislature in 1785, Butler protested his defeat on the grounds that he ought to have been elected because he was the richest man on the island, damned his opponent's supporters as Yankees and Scotsmen and petulantly threatened to leave the country if the vote was not declared invalid. The following year he actually did leave the country — not out of pique but to escape arrest for defrauding the customs by exporting foreign (presumably American) whale oil on the pretense that it was British.

When he learned that Butler had fled to Boston, Captain McGill charged him with absconding in order to escape paying his debts. Rather than allow the courts to seize his property and hand it over to his creditors, Butler returned to New Brunswick, where he was arrested on the customs charge and sentenced to spend three months in jail and pay a fine of £500. After breaking out of jail and being recaptured he was released, probably through the intercession of Sir John Wentworth.

Rebecca Butler wrote to a friend:

> I have of late experienced so much distress, and suffered so
> many tortures of mind, that I seem almost callous to misfor-
> tune, and these things, the mere idea of which would in earlier
> times have made me shudder, now seem familiar, and almost
> stupefy my senses with repeated shock, every one of which
> comes armed with sharper stings than the former.

Meanwhile, in 1785 there took place the first murder known
to have occurred on Campobello. A Loyalist ex-soldier named
John Dunbar killed his wife in a drunken rage and hid her
body in a pork barrel. They lived in a cove facing the Bay of
Fundy, at the foot of a hill subsequently known as Dunbar's
Hill. In his confession, Dunbar said that his wife had hidden
some gold in the hill and refused to tell him where it was. He
was tried and sentenced to death at St. Andrews and, although he twice escaped, was finally hanged there. It is said
that for years afterwards people searched Dunbar's Hill for
gold.

*David Owen, the second
Principal Proprietary: a
bitter exile from England
where once he had been a
tutor to a future prime
minister.*

Chapter five ❧ 1787-1834

> Nor has the world a better thing
>> Though one should search it 'round,
> Than thus to live one's own sole king,
>> Upon one's own sole ground.

—*from The Old Squire by Wilfrid Scawen Blunt*

A portrait in oils of David Owen, the second Principal Proprietary of Campobello and a nephew of Captain William Owen, known on the island during his lifetime as the Squire, hangs in the public library at Welshpool, a village that he founded on the shores of Harbour de L'Outre. It is a portrait of a young man in the gown and with the mortar board hat of a master of arts and senior fellow of Trinity College, Cambridge. There is little life in the portrait: it is as if the unknown artist had worked from a wax mannequin rather than a living model. But there is an interesting contrast between the arrogant set of the head, the disdainful mouth and jaw, and the languid position of the body, the sensual brown eyes. It is not hard to imagine this man behaving like the villainous landlord in a Victorian melodrama or playing the fiddle at country dances, both of which he in fact did.

David Owen had taken deacon's orders in the church at a time when to be a member of the English clergy was not so much a matter of having a religious vocation as of belonging to one of the very few professions regarded as suitable to a gentleman. In keeping with the family tradition he sailed as a chaplain and secretary in the Royal Navy and saw action against the French. After he went to Campobello to claim his inheritance, his enemies, who were legion, whispered that he had found it convenient to leave the navy because his courage had been called in question, and that he had left England either because of his resentment at not having received a lucrative appointment in the church or because his weakness for wine and women threatened the family with disgrace.

Squire Owen first set foot on the island in 1787 at the age of thirty-three and, during his long and disputatious reign as Principal Proprietary of Campobello, there came to be a great many people who felt they had ample reason to believe the worst of him. They said that the original Owen grant had been forfeited in 1784 and that it had been reaffirmed in 1787 only because of David Owen's friendship with the Prime Minister, William Pitt, whose tutor he had been at Cambridge. They were infuriated, understandably enough, by the irony of David Owen claiming successfully that his family had complied with the conditions of the grant by "cultivating and improvement as to have freedom from forfeiture" when it was they — the people whom he treated as squatters and trespassers — who had done all the cultivating and improving. Small wonder that they said that "his meanness was as low as his pride was great," that he was "a great gossip and disposed to listen to everyone who would flatter him," and that he was a man of "deep intrigue and inveterate prejudices."

The courts in Halifax ruled that the Wilson sheriff's sale in 1783 to Charles Morris had been invalid since Captain Owen was dead at the time of the sale and no judgment could be taken against a dead man. David Owen came to Campobello and moved into his uncle's old Man O'War house. Later he was to build a new house, near the site of the present Roosevelt cottage, and to call it *Tyn-y-Coed* (house in the woods), after the family seat in Wales.

A letter from Squire Owen to one of his former associates at Trinity College dated April 8, 1789, suggests that if he was, as he has been accused of being, a "hard man," he was also a man with considerable intellectual curiosity. He tells his friend Hailstone that he is "in some degree concerned" in the "ancient offices of priest and king" and is "at present attending the sessions as a magistrate of the inferior court of common pleas." He promises to send samples of "many curious plants" and to report on the results of his study of "the Indian practice of physick," they being "very expert in applying herbs and plants" including "Labrador tea, sassaparilla, ginsing, Indian potatoes, Indian wildpea and American clover." He says he will also send some stuffed birds. And he reports that "the inhabitants are busy in boiling sugar from the sap of the beech [sic] tree. It is the most beautiful in colour and taste and smell I ever saw. It exceeds the cane sugar in every respect. It is astonishing what quantity a tree gives."

But it would have taken more than sugar to sweeten the bitter brew that David Owen expected the islanders to swallow when he rode his horse up to their doors and served them with notices of ejectment. The struggle over property rights on Campobello was so fierce and so prolonged that even today Mrs. Willa Enos, seventy-five, said to be the last

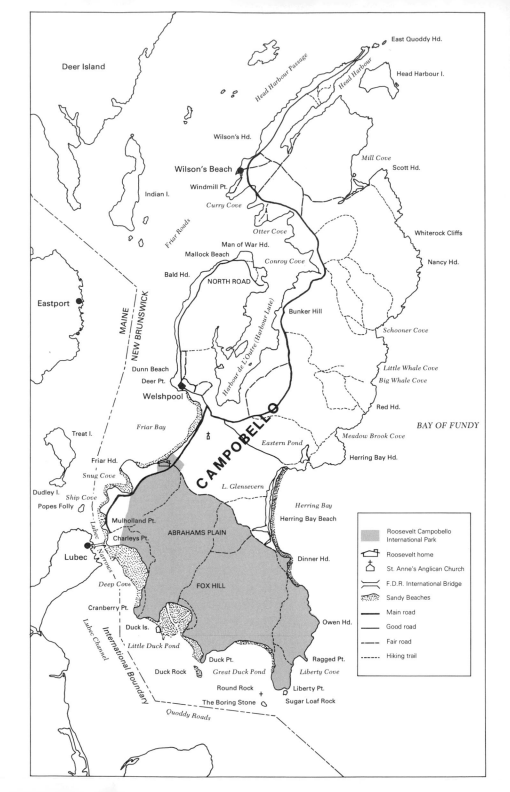

Deer Island

East Quoddy Hd.

Head Harbour Passage

Head Harbour

Head Harbour I.

Wilson's Hd.

Mill Cove

Scott Hd.

Wilson's Beach

Windmill Pt.

Indian I.

Curry Cove

Whiterock Cliffs

Friar Roads

Otter Cove

Nancy Hd.

Man of War Hd.

Mallock Beach

Conroy Cove

Bald Hd.

NORTH ROAD

MAINE

NEW BRUNSWICK

Eastport

Bunker Hill

Schooner Cove

Harbour de L'Outre (Harbour Lute)

Little Whale Cove

Big Whale Cove

Dunn Beach

Deer Pt.

Welshpool

Red Hd.

CAMPOBELLO

BAY OF FUNDY

Friar Bay

Treat I.

Eastern Pond

Meadow Brook Cove

Herring Bay Hd.

Friar Hd.

Snug Cove

L. Glensevern

Dudley I.

Ship Cove

Popes Folly

Herring Bay

Herring Bay Beach

Mulholland Pt.

ABRAHAMS PLAIN

Charleys Pt.

Dinner Hd.

Lubec

Deep Cove

FOX HILL

Cranberry Pt.

Owen Hd.

Duck Is.

Little Duck Pond

Duck Pt.

Ragged Pt.

Duck Rock

Great Duck Pond

Liberty Cove

Round Rock

Liberty Pt.

The Boring Stone

Sugar Loaf Rock

Quoddy Roads

Lubec Narrows

International Boundary

Lubec Channel

	Roosevelt Campobello International Park
	Roosevelt home
	St. Anne's Anglican Church
	F.D.R. International Bridge
	Sandy Beaches
	Main road
	Good road
	Fair road
	Hiking trail

52

descendant of Robert Wilson still living on the island, will mutter darkly: "There are people around here that may be in for a surprise one of these days; people don't always own what they think they own."

The situation was further complicated by the questionable transactions of Gilliam Butler, now out of jail and once again doing business on Campobello in association with Captain Storrow.

In December 1788, Squire Owen summoned the sheriff, John Dunn of St. Andrews, to evict the Butlers and Storrows and to seize their personal belongings in lieu of rent. Only Rebecca Butler, Nancy Storrow and their children were at home at the time. Prudently they had hidden their silver in the woods. Finding herself homeless, Mrs. Butler hired a small vessel to carry her family and her remaining effects to Rhode Island, while Mrs. Storrow, who seems to have been as rugged and obstinate as Mary Wilson, went with her four children in a small boat to nearby Frederic Island where she took refuge with the United States customs collector Lewis Frederic Delesdernier. Claiming that he had been defrauded David Owen assembled a "party of armed men and in a boat proceeded to Frederic Island with an intention of seizing the few articles of property which remained in her possession. . . . This was opposed by Mr. Delesdernier, who with a loaded musket defended his home and would not suffer any one to enter. Owen directed the sheriff and armed posse to force an entrance. The sheriff distrusted his own power to proceed, and the armed men refused to act unless by the sheriff's order. Finding nothing could be done Owen proposed returning to Campobello, and on the way to the boat, meeting a cow belonging to Nancy, which was the chief dependence for the children's food—the dastardly wretch caused her to be taken over to Campobello."

According to Nancy Storrow's own account the Squire said that he would not have acted as he had done if it had not been for her "damnable tongue," and it is obvious from her surviving letters that the lady had a taste for invective. He had said that she was a former milliner who could not keep her tongue between her teeth. She retorted that he was an "unprincipled wretch" guilty of "lawless depredations" whom she hoped to drive "raving mad." It was with great satisfaction that she described a violent encounter between this "unaccountable oddity" and her friend Captain Christopher Hatch. Also involved in this altercation was the woman, Hannah Smith, who was to be the Squire's mistress and companion for forty years.

You know there has been blood shed between Hatch and him . . . and [it]gave out that his [Owen's] skull was fractured, which idea gave rise to a great deal of wit among the bucks of St. Andrews, for that his head was hurt, say they, everyone but himself knew long ago. The cause of the quarrel was Owen thought proper, after a great deal of general abuse of the whole family, to call Mrs. Hatch and Miss Talman by very genteel names, and desired the person to whom he addressed his discourse to make a minute of what he said, which he did, and immediately took to inform Hatch, who soon after went to Owen's house, accompany'd by his brother Hawes, and a Capt. Walker, of a ship laying at Snug Cove. Hatch taxed Owen with the fact, who at first equivocated, but at last said that he had made use of such expressions and told Hatch to make the most of it. They then proceeded to blows, and Hatch gave Owen's head one or two openings, he showed a pistol and challenged Owen to produce his, which however he declined. The Vestal of friar's bay fought most valiantly [the reader can practically see the feline glint in Nancy Storrow's eyes as she applied this epithet to Hannah Smith], she cuffed Hatch, pulled his hair, and in short performed the part of a heroine, till the sight of Owen's blood quite over-powered her, and she fainted on the floor.

Captain Hatch, a Loyalist soldier who had been wounded and commended for gallantry, was taken into custody together with his brother, Hawes Hatch, and his friend, Captain Thomas Walker, and the three were charged at St. Andrews with assault and battery. The outcome of the trial is not known, for the records have been lost. In any event it was impossible for Captain Hatch to continue to live on Campobello. He abandoned his house and store on the island and moved to St. Andrews where eventually he "built himself a large brick house, where he lived in much elegance and dispensed a royal hospitality." He was also made a magistrate. The Captain was popular in St. Andrews, where it was apparently felt that nobody who bloodied David Owen's head could be all bad.

Owen was less successful in his attempts to drive out the Wilsons. In a suit heard at St. Andrews in 1790 Mary Wilson claimed that her family's rights had been recognized by Captain Owen. The jury ruled in her favour although the Squire later maintained that they had done so only after they "retired to a tavern and liquor was furnished through a back window." He also charged that eleven of the jurors had been on his side but that "the foreman, one Frost, who was connected in some manner with the defendant, held out, and next day in the open street he boasted that he had worn out the jury and would have kept them till the verdict suited his own purpose."

The Wilson settlement remained, although David Owen and his successors never ceased to refer to it as "the Wilson Encroachment." The two communities settled into a policy of sullen co-existence punctuated by legal action or violence — as when in 1816 the Squire tried to evict a certain Jonathan Parker, claiming that he had lent him money to build a house and had not been repaid, and that Parker did not pay his rent.

The house was to be transferred to the Squire's favourite, Charles Hatheway, surveyor, deputy collector and captain of militia. But when Hatheway, accompanied by the sheriff, went to claim the property he was attacked by a crowd led by Sarah Wilson, Mary's daughter-in-law, who brandished a sword that had been carried by Robert Wilson during the French and Indian War. Parker kept the house. Later Sarah Wilson, carrying the same sword, led a party of women armed with butter clappers and pots of boiling water in an attack on the Squire's fence builders. The Squire must have relented toward Jonathan Parker, for he later made him the first licensed liquor-seller on the island.

In view of his difficulties it is not surprising that the Squire wished to rid himself of the island. At one point an agreement was signed whereby his brother-in-law, Thomas Jones of Montgomeryshire, would buy the Principal Proprietorship for £2,000 down and another £2,000 in five years. The deal fell through but the Squire kept the downpayment on the grounds that he had been subjected to extraordinary personal expenses in evicting trespassers and that the other members of the family in England and Wales had refused to pay their share of these expenses. Later he made a fruitless attempt to sell the island to the Crown, explaining that he found his daily life and his real estate a burden to him.

In 1796 David Owen became a member of the New Brunswick Legislative Assembly. There he sought to maintain the semi-independent status of his little principality, arguing that the Crown had neither the right to tax the island nor the right to call up its men for military duty without his consent.

In the early years of the nineteenth century world events affected Campobello more dramatically than they had ever done before or are ever likely to do again. The British Empire was fighting its seemingly interminable war with Napoleonic

A letter written by David Owen, characteristic of him in its assertion that his town is being "greviously oppressed" and his "person property and reputation .. grossly abused."

REV'D SIR,

The Society in London for propagating the Gospel has requested, that I would make my communications, respecting this place, through the Bishop of Nova Scotia.

In compliance therewith, I now acquaint you, as his Commissary in this province that, subsequent to their appointment of Mr. James Berry, as a schoolmaster on Campo Bello, in 1788, a person who had been employed by me with a salary of thirty pounds a year before he received the salary of fifteen pounds sterling from the society; and of Mr. Green, whom I furnished with a good dwelling house and Farm; and who, on Mr. Berry's going to Saint Andrews, drew the salary for a short time; no permanent establishment has been by me made for schools, as I heretofore intended; and that, unless the peace of the Town be restored, and the Inhabitants be not oppressed and driven away from the Island, as they are at present, I must give up every idea of establishing permanent schools thereon; while such evils exist—I mean, by granting lands for the purpose or by other *donations in perpetuity.* The Reverend Mr. James Jones, whom I recommended as a missionary, when I recommended Mr. Berry as a schoolmaster; and to whom and others the society offered a Donation of forty pounds sterling a year, as soon as the Inhabitants should subscribe; and a Glebe and Church be fixed and appropriated, soon left this place without officiating. I was at great expense on his account for passage from England, and other matters; and was wholly disappointed by his conduct here—To encourage Religious Establishments within the County, I promised to give fifty dollars towards the erecting of the first place of public worship in each Town or Parish therein—One Parish only, *Saint Davids,* applied for and received the Donation.

Desirous of having a corporate Body of Wardens and Vestry under the act of assembly, wherein to vest property for the *permanent use of a church and schools,* I obtained an act of the Legislature of the province, in the year eighteen hundred and three; to constitute the Island of Campo Bello, with its appurtenances in the County of Charlotte, a distinct Town and Parish; by the name of the Town and Parish of Campo Bello; and soon thereafter built a Chapel, at my own expense, in a central situation; which has occasionally been used by the Missionary at Saint Andrews and others for public worship; and is now kept for that use. It has also been used, at different times, for a school house. It will contain about two hundred hearers; has a Bell and Steeple; is in good repair and rather a handsome little building.

Last autumn, Sir Howard Douglas, our Commander in Chief, and Lieut. Governor declared his wishes to me at Campo Bello; That there might be a Church on Campo Bello and also on Deer Island; to be served by one Missionary—I then offered to build a Church on Campo Bello, at my own expense; provided the Islands were made a County, separate from Charlotte, within a year; according to the petitions to his Majesty and the directions to His Excellency to report thereon; which I expected would be both prompt and favorable—His Excellency was afterwards told by me, that I had built a Chapel, many years before; and the building was shewn to him from my dwelling house.

That offer I now look upon as cancelled—This Town is grievously oppressed; my person, property and reputation has been and still is grossly abused.—Ten families left the place lately and others must and will leave it —moreover, unless speedy relief be obtained, I purpose to abandon a property, which might this day have been worth one hundred and fifty thousand pounds sterling; and where I have spent thirty eight years of my life; with above forty thousand dollars in my endeavours to create and establish a flourishing settlement.

However, while the society receives this account of the causes, which now operate here to prevent what was expected to have been established in support of Religion; I have to mention, that, with a view of having a regular Clergyman near the place, who might occasionally perform service in the Chapel, I gave a liberal sum towards the building of a Congregational Church at Lubec (a Town contiguous to Campo Bello) as well as at Grand Manan; which Parish, with Campo Bello and West Isles, I hoped, by this time, would have been a separate County from Charlotte: the chief, if not the only means, to relieve me and the Inhabitants from the evils, which we suffer.

The Society will therefore discard any apprehension, that I solicited its aid without real intentions to promote the object of its Institution, as long as there appeared any hopes of that security to my possessions here, which I had a right to expect—and without which, it would be absurd in me to attempt to assign a Glebe, School-House lots or do, at present, other public Acts of that or any other kind whatever.

I am, Rev'd Sir,

Your obed't humble Serv't,

D. OWEN.

The Rev'd MR. BEST,

    Commissary, &c. &c. &c.

CAMPO BELLO, 21st FEB. 1826. It being necessary, that Copies of the above letter should be furnished to the Missionaries and others concerned, as well in this province as in England; it is now printed for that purpose.
D. OWEN.

France. The Emperor had said that an army travels on its stomach. The British knew that he was right. In a move unprecedented in the annals of war they put the entire continent of Europe under blockade. Cut off from some of its best customers, the United States determined to give Britain a taste of its own medicine. In 1807 Congress passed the Embargo Act forbidding American ships to embark for any foreign port. Quickly, Eastport, Maine, only two miles from Campobello, became one of the busiest towns in the United States. Smuggling became Campobello's chief industry. The islanders said: "That's why fogs were made."

Kate Gannett Wells writes:

> Provincial trade was peculiar. British vessels, laden with gypsum and grindstones, because they came from ports not open to American vessels, sailed to the frontier out on the lines and transferred their cargo to American vessels waiting there. Slaves from Norfolk, Virginia, were sent to some neutral island, and from there transported to an English ship, again out on the lines, and then carried to the West Indies.

In 1809 the United States repealed the Embargo Act and substituted the Non-Intercourse Act which allowed American ships to trade with any country except England and France. Soon it was commonly said that Eastport was home to the fastest ships in the world — ships that could sail from Maine to Sweden in three or four hours and sometimes make the same trip twice in one day. After all, "It was but a moment's work to transform Yankees or Bluenoses into natives of Stockholm or Upsalla." The goods smuggled included silk, wool, cotton and metals. From Eastport they were carried by wagon up the Penobscot River and then to Portland, Boston and New York.

On June 1, 1812, the conflicting economic interests of Britain and the United States boiled over into war. The War of 1812

Head Harbour, Campobello.

was both an epilogue to the American Revolution and a footnote to the Napoleonic Wars. Most of the fighting took place on the Great Lakes, in what are now the state of Michigan and the province of Ontario. In this curious war the people of New England and the Maritime provinces generally treated each other as neutrals, at least on land, although a New Brunswick regiment — the 104th Regiment of Foot — achieved fame by marching in winter from Fredericton to Quebec City, and later taking up arms against the Americans at the battles of Sackett's Harbour, Lundy's Lane and Fort Erie.

Four years before the outbreak of hostilities the United States had aroused indignation in the Maritime provinces by building Fort Sullivan at Eastport. In the month following the declaration of war the fort and town fell to the British without a shot being fired:

> On July 11th a fleet was seen coming round Campobello by Head Harbour which at first was supposed to be a fleet of merchant men or lumber ships, bound to St. Andrews under the

convoy of a frigate. When it arrived as far as Indian Island a sloop of war was dispatched ahead, with a flag of truce. A boat landed from her with an officer who repaired to the fort with a summons to surrender; five minutes were allowed the commanding officer (Major Putnam) to consider . . . he declared his determination to disregard the summons, and to fire upon the ships . . . several of the principal inhabitants had now repaired to the fort . . . and strenuously opposed such a course . . . they stated . . . that all resistance on his part would be in vain; that a force would be landed and overpower him almost before he could harm a single vessel of the fleet with his small battery . . . and that to save the town from destruction was his imperative duty. . . . Major Putnam finally consented to accept the terms offered to him and accordingly struck his colours . . . in less than an hour from the time of the summons, fifteen barges, containing five hundred troops, had landed and the 64-gun ship, after landing her troops, anchored under Campobello. . . .

"I could have taken it with a gun, brig and my own militia," the Squire commented derisively.

Eastport was occupied by the British for two years, one of the British commanders being Sir Thomas Hardy, the man to whom the dying Lord Nelson whispered either "Kiss me, Hardy," or "Kismet, Hardy." The inhabitants were told that if they took the oath of allegiance to King George they would be treated as friendly civilians. This they readily agreed to do. After which they proceeded to go about their business pretty much as usual until the Treaty of Ghent in 1814 brought them back under the jurisdiction of the United States. In fact they were probably more content with the presence of the British army and navy than was David Owen who, during the occupation, bombarded both the British commander and the New Brunswick government with complaints about the behaviour of the jacktars and lobsterbacks who made off with his sheep, took over certain of his empty houses, set fire to his store, and fired their muskets so indiscriminately that they killed one of his pigs and wounded another. He demanded without much success that such "calamities of warfare" be "repelled from the doors of my people."

In June 1829, the Squire made a will in which he bequeathed the island to his cousins, Edward William Campbell Rich Owen and William Fitzwilliam Owen, sons of the first Principal Proprietary. He also made provision for Hannah Smith in tribute to her "long and faithful service," and for two young men, David Owen Russel and Price Owen Flagg, who may have been his illegitimate sons. The following December he died and his body was placed in a lead coffin filled with spirits and shipped across the Atlantic for burial in his native Montgomeryshire. The islanders preferred to believe that the sailors drank the spirits and threw the corpse into the sea.

Five years later, death came to Hannah Smith. Thanks to the Squire's bequest, she was one of the wealthiest persons on the island. She left almost all of her small fortune to the British and Foreign Bible Society.

Admiral William Owen, the third Principal Proprietary, who styled himself "the Hermit of Passamaquoddy."

Chapter six ❧ 1835-1857

At fifty-one my worldly ambitions were barred by corruption in high places. At sixty-one I became the Hermit.

— Admiral William Fitzwilliam Owen

There arrived on Campobello in September 1835 the third Principal Proprietary, Admiral William Fitzwilliam Owen, sailor, cartographer and amateur theologian, whose fancy it was to regard the island as a place of exile and to style himself the Hermit of Passamaquoddy. By his own account the Admiral was a latter-day Robinson Crusoe. Actually he brought with him not only his wife and two daughters, Portia, sixteen, and Cornelia, fifteen, but two shiploads of settlers, cattle and supplies to join the four hundred people already living there —people described by his agent as a "miserable remnant of poor fishermen."

This younger, Manchester-born son of old Captain Owen was now sixty-one and had been on the books of the Royal Navy since the age of four. In his book *The Quoddy Hermit*, a potpourri of philosophical meanderings and fictionalized autobiography, he says that his earliest memory was of eating from the head of a dead horse in a town whose food had been cut off by a besieging army. At five he was taken from his mother, supposedly Sarah Haslem, by his father's old friend Sir Thomas Rich (the Quoddy Hermit says that when Sir Thomas asked him what was his last name he answered: "I don't know — but if you want to know you can ask in the barracks. Mother can tell you.")

He was put in a public school in Wales. Later:

> I was put out on board with a writing master, and almost starved; by God's providence a butcher's wife was raised up to save me from impending miserable death, and at seven years old, I found myself an inmate in the family of a widow, with five young children, a farmer, whose husband had lately hung himself, where the plenty of the land was before me. . . . Whilst here, I became a prey to a scrofulous disease — the supposed result of a sudden transition from starvation to plenty, which lasted seven or more years. . . . When questioned about my father and mother, I was used to answer with all sincerity and simplicity, "I never had any" — so that I was known at school, jocularly I suppose, until I was thirteen, as the boy who never had father or mother. About ten, however, I had a sensible mark of the earthly pre-existence of someone who claimed to be my father, for I had a suit of scarlet and a cocked hat, said to have been made [the suit] from an old coat of my father's. I learned too, that he had been an officer of some renown, mutilated like Nelson by the loss of an arm and eye.

The pathetic little boy in the scarlet coat and cocked hat himself served under Nelson when he became a man. Among

Nelson's correspondence there is a letter to Lieutenant William Fitzwilliam Owen, commanding His Majesty's fire vessel *Nancy*. Dated October 2, 1801, it expresses "entire confidence" in Owen's "energy and zeal" and assigns him to a secret mission, that of attempting to set fire to the French flotilla in harbour at Boulogne, where Napoleon was believed to be assembling his forces in preparation for an invasion of England. The letter is accompanied by a memorandum in which Nelson says: "It is my direction that no officer whatever senior to Lieutenant Owen, commanding the *Nancy*, do call on him for his orders, they being of a secret nature."

Admiral Owen's career, like that of many another naval officer in the heyday of British imperialism, carried him to every corner of the world and involved him in exploration and colonial administration as well as in warfare. He fought the French, the Spanish, the Dutch and the Ashanti. For two years he was a prisoner of the French in Mauritius. He served in the West Indies, Indonesia, India, Africa and North America. He explored the Maldive Islands, discovered a channel on the west coast of Sumatra, surveyed the east coast of Africa and the Great Lakes. Owen Sound, Ontario, was named for him. A settlement was planted under his direction on Fernando Póo, and he served as that island's Governor. Commented the Quoddy Hermit: "The almost uninterrupted nature of my public services left me little leisure to pursue my disposition to acquire spiritual knowledge." He gave free rein to that disposition during his years on Campobello, recording the results in the form of dialogues between himself and three imaginary friends named Academicus, Rusticus and Theophilus.

On the high crest of Deer Point, at the western end of Welshpool, overlooking the bay, using the frame of the Squire's *Tyn-y-Coed* and building materials brought from

England, the Admiral built a house which still stands:

> Two large low rooms opened on each side of the front door; a most comfortable staircase leading from the small entry to equally pleasant rooms in the second storey. Damask and Indian muslin curtains shaded the many-paned windows; heavy mahogany and redwood chairs, sofas, and tables furnished its apartments; great logs on tall andirons burned in the monster fireplaces; sacred maps hung around the evening parlour and the dining room carpet was said to have been a gift of the King of Prussia.

The Admiral planted English oaks, placed the sundial of his vessel in the garden, set up two Spanish cannon that he had captured, and erected near the shore a replica of the quarterdeck of a man-o'-war. When he was not in conversation with Academicus, Rusticus and Theophilus, it was the Admiral's practice to don his full dress uniform and pace up and down his landlocked quarterdeck.

Admiral Owen's house. The Admiral and his Lady dined under silver candelabra from silver- and gold-lined dishes, but suffered a good deal from the cold.

At first Lady Owen and the girls did not like their new home. They longed for England. As a gesture of protest Lady Owen refused to put down her stair carpet, implying that she did not intend to stay for long, and the girls complained that in winter they had to sleep with cats to keep warm. But matters improved. The Admiral and his Lady dined under silver candelabra, from silver and gold-lined dishes, and accompanied their meal with imported wines. He bought a coach and four with which to carry out inspections of his domain.

In the years between the Squire's death and the Admiral's arrival, the island had been administered by agents, one of whom had demanded so high a percentage of the fishermen's profits that they refused to fish. Short of fertile soil, and far from the markets for farm produce, Campobello was becoming more and more an island of fishermen.

A weir (pronounced *ware*) is essentially a pen set up near the shore into which the fish, mostly small herring, swim at high tide and are trapped as the tide recedes. The first weirs were erected off Campobello in 1840. Fastened to stakes driven into the seabed they were walled in the old days by intertwined brush; today nylon twine netting is used. The fishermen remove the fish from the weir by dropping a weighted net, called a purse-seine, vertically into the water and bringing its ends together. Formerly the weirs were given names like ships, and it is said that one of them, called *I Am Alone*, was so christened by one of two partners who felt that he had done more than his share of the work of building it.

By 1850 there were twenty-one weirs off Campobello employing one hundred boys and men, fifty boats employing another one hundred, and eleven larger fishing vessels with a total complement of fifty-two boys and men—this out of a total population of eight hundred and sixty-five. In 1861 the islanders sold $66,545 worth of cod, haddock, hake, pollock,

The fireplace in Admiral Owen's house. The dining room carpet was said to have been a gift of the King of Prussia.

mackerel and herring, the equivalent of about $250,000 in today's currency. A century later, Winslow Newman, the first Superintendent of the Roosevelt Campobello International Park, could tell a visitor: "When they call a man a farmer on Campobello, it's not a compliment."

At one point the Admiral seems to have been so carried away by his imagination that he dreamt of transforming his domain into another industrial Lancashire. On June 1, 1839, there was incorporated the Campobello Mill and Manufacturing Company, with a capital of $400,000, and with the Admiral as its President. Its stated purpose was the "erecting, using and employing" of "all descriptions of mills, mill-dams, fulling and carding machinery" and it was claimed that as a site for manufacturing operations Campobello would "have a decided advantage over any other spot in British America." Nothing came of it.

It was this same year 1839 that Cornelia Owen married John James Robinson. In keeping with the traditions of the family into which he married, the Admiral's new son-in-law had been a midshipman in the Royal Navy when he was thirteen years old. He had served off the coast of Africa (where he

The Franklin D. Roosevelt summer residence on Campobello, the
President's "beloved island," is today a focal point of the park.

Opened in 1962, the Roosevelt International Bridge symbolizes what President John Kennedy called the "bond of friendship" between Canada and the United States.

assisted in the capture of two slave ships), in the West Indies
and the Mediterranean, and rose to the rank of captain before
retiring at thirty-four because of ill health and taking up residence on Campobello in 1845. The Admiral's elder daughter,
Portia, had married before Cornelia, in 1836, and had gone to
live on another island — Jersey, in the English Channel.

Thwarted in his attempt to emulate his kinsman, the indus-
trialist and Utopian thinker Robert Owen, the Admiral turned
his attention to government. In 1844 he was appointed to the
New Brunswick Legislative Council, and made a justice of the
inferior court of common pleas, a justice of the peace and a
commissioner for solemnizing marriages. He caused to be appointed to Campobello such officials as "commissioners and
surveyors of highways, overseers of poor and of fisheries, as-
sessors, trustees of schools, inspectors of fish for home consumption and for export, for smoked herring and boxes . . .
cullers of staves, fence viewers, and hog reeves, and surveyors of lumber and cordwood, lest that which should
properly be used for the purposes of building or export be
consumed on andirons or in the kitchen."

The Principal Proprietary issued a decree forbidding swine

and sheep to run wild, as they had previously done. He established a fine of five shillings for every pig not ringed and yoked. Fines were imposed on violators of the monopoly held by the official ferryman who carried passengers and goods between the island and Eastport. It was ordered that "all dogs of six months old and older shall be considered of sufficient age to pay the tax [sic]." The Admiral founded his own bank and issued his own currency, which was used among other things to pay those who worked on the roads and bridges. Such workers were paid "at the rate of 1.12\frac{1}{2}$ per man per day, the day being ten hours of good and conscientious work for man or yoke of oxen."

Regulations governing animal on Campobello, passed by the Principal Proprietary, soon afte his arrival on the island.

Nor was the Principal Proprietary indifferent to what would today be known as social services. He arranged to have a sixteen-year-old girl trained as a nurse. Her work seems to have consisted mostly of midwifery, of which she said in later years: "My general price was three dollars, but when folks was no better off than I, I turned in and asked nothin'."

During this period there existed on Campobello and elsewhere in Atlantic Canada a macabre practice known as the "auctioning of the poor." Paupers, whether orphan children or dotards, were sold at public auction to the lowest bidder: in other words, they were given into the hands of whoever asked the least money in return for providing them with bed and board for a year. A husky twelve-year-old and a feeble octogenarian might bring the same low price, say $50, because in one case the bidder planned to make sure that the lad more than earned his keep and in the other the bidder was gambling that the old man would die before he had consumed $50 worth of food. If the boy proved to be less productive than was anticipated he could be enlivened with a tonic of strap oil and boot grease, as the saying went, and if the old man persisted wrong-headedly in clinging to life he could be made to

Regulations

For preventing Trespasses in the Parish of Campobello, passed April Sessions,

1836

Ordered, That no swine be allowed to run at large in the Parish of Campobello unless sufficiently yoked and ringed.

Ordered, That no Cattle or Sheep be allowed to run at large without proper marks to designate their owner, which marks are to be regularly registered by the Town Clerk under the penalty of two and six pence for each beast excepting sheep, for which the fine is limited by 6 Wm. 4. Chap. 29 to six pence.

Ordered, That the owner of Sheep grazing or running at large shall be amenable for all trespasses on enclosed land.

Ordered, That neither horses, Cattle, Swine, Sheep, Ram, or Goats be allowed to run at large without licence from the proprietor of the uninclosed lands, if so found shall be liable to be taken up and impounded by the Hog Reeves or Pound keepers and the owner or owners subjected to be fined for each and every horse, cattle, or swine, the sum of five shillings and for every sheep, one shilling with such additional charges and expences as are authorised to be exacted by the Act of the Assembly in such case made and provided.

Ordered, That all fines to be levied under these regulations shall be paid over to the Overseers of the Poor, unless otherwise provided by the Act of Assembly.

Ordered, That no geese be allowed to run at large in the Par unless sufficiently yoked so as to prevent them tr cribed by the Act of Assembly in such case ma

St. Anne's Anglican Church, erected in 1855. The Admiral offered three years of free pasturage for the cattle of Episcopalians.

sleep in the barn where the draughts were almost certain to hasten his departure from this vale of tears. On the other hand, a bidder might demand as much as $100 for a child too small for heavy work or an old person known to possess sound lungs and a hearty appetite.

Like his predecessors the Admiral regularly conducted services according to the rituals of the Church of England. Most of the original Loyalists had been Anglicans, but large numbers of their descendants had become Baptists, chiefly as a result of an evangelical movement known as the New Light, founded by Henry Alline, a Nova Scotia preacher and mystic (later made famous by William James in his *The Varieties of Religious Experience*). In 1854 a New Light congregation calling itself the Christian Church of Campobello authorized its pastor, Elder Peter Malloch, to unite it with the Free Christian Baptist Conference of New Brunswick. A portrait of Peter Malloch hangs in the present United Baptist Church at Wilson's Beach. On Campobello in the Admiral's day the Baptists, centred at Wilson's Beach, outnumbered the Anglicans, centred at Welshpool, by more than two to one, and the discrepancy might have been greater if the Principal Proprietary had not offered three years of free pasturage for the cattle of those who belonged to the "Church Episcopal Congregation."

The Admiral was responsible for the erection in 1855 of St. Anne's Anglican Church, in which services are still held. The block of stone from which the baptismal font was carved in Italy was taken from the Church of the Knights Templar in

Malta by the Admiral's son-in-law, Captain John James
Robinson of the Royal Navy. The chancel carpet, altar vest-
ments, stoles and chalice veils in green, white, crimson and
purple were worked by the Admiral's daughters and grand-
daughters. St. Anne's looks little different today than when
the Admiral worshipped there, except that on the wall behind
the back pew there has been erected a bronze plaque reading:

To The Glory of God
In Memory of
Franklin Delano Roosevelt
1882-1945
Honorary Vestryman of
St. Anne's Church

The Admiral officiated at family services every morning and
evening, but in this instance his piety was tempered consider-
ably by his practicality — he insisted that the maids continue
with their sewing except during prayers. Being, like his cousin
David before him, both priest and king, the Admiral did not
hesitate to revise the Bible; whenever he came to a passage
that made mention of the "wiles of the devil," he changed the
word "wiles" to "methodisms."

Not that the islanders spent all their time at work or prayer.
In 1851 the first fish fair was held, attended by "doctors,
lawyers, ministers both ecclesiastical and governmental, and
ladies all slippered for the dance" who watched "the fastest
sailing boats spread their canvas wings to fly over the waves
of Quoddy." An ageing and wistful islander was later to recall
these as "the good old days when West India rum flowed like
milk and West India sugar was sweet as honey, when everybody treated everybody, when everybody got merry, when
everybody would sing, swear, dance and fight."

Lady Owen died in 1852. The Admiral remarried in 1855 at the age of eighty-one, in a belated attempt to shake off the role of the Quoddy Hermit that he had created for himself twenty years before. He had decided in his old age that the company of one Widow Nicholson in Saint John was more congenial than that of his old companions, Academicus, Rusticus and Theophilus. Death came to him in the New Brunswick port city on November 3, 1857. Kate Gannett Wells writes with her usual grandiloquence:

> The boat that bore him back from Saint John for the last time to his hermitage ran aground; for the great falling tides bade him wait, even in the pomp of death, until it was their hour to bear him aloft on his oft-trod pier.

The Admiral's body lies in a surprisingly modest grave near the entrance to St. Anne's Churchyard. The most striking feature of the Owen family plot is a Celtic cross erected in memory of the Admiral's grandson, Lieutenant John Hemery Robinson-Owen, who died aboard H.M.S. *Endymion* in 1870 and was buried in the Sea of Japan.

What a strange life he had lived, and what a curious man he had been, this Admiral who had begun as a starving waif and, by his own account, an "ulcered Lazarus," a victim of scrofula, that disfiguring disease once known as "the King's Evil" because it was believed that it could be cured by the touch of a king. His portrait in oils and a wax bust of him are on display in the Welshpool Public Library. He was an ugly man, to be sure, with the prominent and distinctive Owen nose; his features in the painting are harsh and coarse, while the bust could be a likeness of Mr. Bumble the beadle in *Oliver Twist*. Yet there's a hint of something more there, at least in the painting, a hint of something kindly, vulnerable and a little mad. "I had much of good and evil," the Admiral himself once wrote of the child that he had been.

Chapter seven ❦ 1857-1881

The captains and the kings depart.

—Kipling

Captain John James Robinson assumed the surname of
Robinson-Owen three years after he settled on Campobello to
comply with the conditions of a bequest from Admiral Sir
Edward William Campbell Rich Owen (he whose father had
dubbed him "the hereditary Prince of Campobello"). Captain
Robinson-Owen was to be the last Principal Proprietary of the
Great Outer Island of Passamaquoddy.

He managed the Owen family's portion of the island after
the death of Lady Owen in 1852, and came to be known
among the islanders as a harsh, avaricious employer and landlord. During the American Civil War of 1861-65 when the

Above: the Emmet, *pleasure craft owned by the Campobello Company.*

Left: First car ferry, capacity 6 cars.

Below: Smoking fish at Welshpool.

Mrs. Flagg enjoys a moment of serenity in the doorway of her home at the narrows.

RULES AND REGULATIONS

For the Ferrymen appointed for the Parish of Campobello, April Sessions 1836.

Ordered, That the following Rules and Rates be observed by the Ferrymen in the said Parish.

1st. The Ferry at Welshpool, and Dennis Beach.

Fare, to or from Eastport,	1s. 3d.
Indian Island,	1s. 0d.
Dear Island, in Indian Island,	1s. 6d.
Putting on board or landing from Steam-boat, calling off Welshpool,	0s. 3d.

2d. The Ferry between Man of War Head and any part of the opposite shore off Campobello, from Wilson's beach to Newman's or back, 1s.

3d. Between any part of Campobello within the Narrows or Ship Cove to Lubec, 7 1-2d. to return for the same unless after the lapse of half an hour.

Ordered, That the Ferrymen on Campobello shall provide themselves with good and sufficient Boats with sails and oars to be kept tight and in good order under penalty of five shillings each day that they fail herein, to be paid to the Overseers of the Poor upon conviction before a Magistrate, unless otherwise provided by the Act of Assembly.

Ordered, That no person shall be allowed to ferry for hire except the persons appointed by the Session for that purpose, under the penalty of 10s. for each offence, half to go to the informer, and half to the licensed Ferrymen, upon conviction before a Magistrate, unless otherwise provided by the Act of Assembly.

Ordered, That if any boat shall bring or take passengers for hire, the proprietor may account to the Ferryman for 6d. per each person, each trip, in which case he shall not be liable to prosecution for any fine, and on this subject the Ferrymen may come to some arrangement with those of Eastport, Indian or Deer Island for their mutual satisfaction, and give passengers any facility for crossing when convenient.

Ordered, That the Ferries to be open for carriage of passengers between 6 o'clock A. M. and sun set, at all other times after to pay double fees.

Ordered, That any Ferryman taking or charging any more than the sums herein directed, shall pay a fine of ten shillings, on conviction before a Magistrate, to be paid to the Overseers of the Poor, unless otherwise provided for by the Act of Assembly in such case made and provided.

Slow but steady mode of travel. St. Anne's Rectory in the background.

Mrs. Mulholland well into her 80's in 1905, busy and active as ever.

value of United States currency was greatly deflated he insisted that his tenants pay their rent in English gold: no paper money was to be accepted. In consequence many of the tenants were unable to meet their payments and lost a part or all of their properties. One man "being old and infirm" was evicted for failing to pay $23, and an old woman was ordered to quit her premises in two weeks, her unpaid debt consisting of $12 for eighteen months rent, $3 for fuel rent, $1 for plastering and $10 for a fence. The middle years of the nineteenth century were hard times on Campobello, a fact that the inhabitants attributed to the Captain's greed and incompetence.

While it is true that Robinson-Owen was far less sympathetic to the people's plight than he might have been, the source of their economic difficulties was much more complex than they believed it to be. In 1854 the five eastern Canadian provinces entered into a reciprocity or free trade agreement with the United States. Thanks to a costly campaign of propaganda and bribery conducted by Israel DeWolfe Andrews, United States Consul in Saint John, the New Brunswick government had been induced to accept a provision allowing Americans to fish within the three-mile limit off the eastern British possessions in North America and to land anywhere "for the purpose of drying their nets and curing their fish." This agreement remained in effect until 1866. Then, starting in Europe and spreading across the Atlantic to the United States and Canada, came the depression of 1873. The island's problems were due more to bad luck than to bad management.

Still, Campobello's situation might have been happier if Captain Robinson-Owen had been as astute as his contemporary, Captain Jabez Pike of Lubec, whose story has been told by his grandson, Sumner Pike, a member of the Roosevelt Campobello International Park Commission and formerly a member of the United States Atomic Energy Commission.

Mr. Pike's family has been established for generations in Lubec, a town that he describes as having been "founded on smuggling and no one frowned upon it except the government." He says that at the time of the American Civil War there was "a fantastically high duty on Canadian wool." So his grandfather "conceived the idea of running in wool from Campobello and mixing it with his own wool." Soon, on the basis of the number of sheep that he owned, Captain Pike was sending "about four hundred pounds of wool per sheep to market."

Then one day Captain Pike heard that a government man was coming over from Machias to see him. He fled to Campobello. "While grandfather was hiding out on Campobello, he had to do something about his brood at home," Mr. Pike says, "so he got himself a two-wheeled cart and started what we might call euphemistically a peddling business. The only thing possibly irregular about it was that nobody bothered to pay any duty. Grandfather would make the rounds of the villages, mainly Welshpool and Wilson's Beach, and take orders. Then at a certain time each day he'd go down to Mulholland Point, where the distance was only about 150 yards over to Lubec, and holler his orders across to father, who was about ten, and Uncle By, who was eight. Father and Uncle By would fill the order from Great-grandfather Moses' store and row it over to grandfather. If they'd made any mistakes he'd bend them over the side of the dory and paddle them so their hearing would improve."

In 1872 Captain Robinson-Owen began trying to sell the island. He could scarcely have chosen a worse time. New York investment houses were being forced to close their doors; railway companies were going into bankruptcy. He was still searching for a buyer two years later when he died in Fredericton, where he had gone to attend a session of the Legis-

lative Assembly of which he was a member. For the following
seven years the island was administered by his widow with
the assistance of his bailiff, John Farmer, who had come to
Campobello with the Admiral as a boy of fifteen. The hard
times continued, although in the late 1870's the situation was
alleviated somewhat by a new industry—rum running. There
were two warehouses on the island where not only rum but
Holland gin, Irish and Scotch whiskies and French wines
were kept in bond until they could be sold and taken aboard
the fishing schooners that came up from Gloucester in fleets
of thirty or forty ostensibly to buy herring.

(Something similar was to take place during the Prohibition
era of the 1920's. While most of the Canadian provinces cur-
tailed or prohibited the sale of intoxicants to their own citizens, several of them, including Quebec and Ontario, permitted breweries and distilleries to manufacture beer or spirits for
export. Others, including New Brunswick, banned the sale of
liquor to local consumers but established bonded warehouses,
crammed with potables; in the three years ending in 1925 almost six million gallons of bonded liquor left Saint John and
Halifax. Canadian vessels also carried liquor from the French
islands of St. Pierre and Miquelon. At one point *The Guardian*
of Charlottetown, Prince Edward Island, warned that so many
fishermen were switching over to rum running that there
were certain to be "evil consequences" to the fishing industry.
Elderly Campobello fishermen tend to change the subject
when asked about the rum running days when Black
Diamond rum could be bought in Jamaica for 17 cents for a
five-gallon keg that could be sold in the United States for $40,
and Campobello fishermen would go out in their small boats
to pick up liquor from the schooners anchored near The
Wolves and carry it to Eastport or Lubec. The island teetotal
tradition is so strong that even in 1974 there was no liquor

store, no tavern and only two restaurants licensed to sell liquor.)

The Owen era ended in 1881 when Mrs. Cornelia Robinson-Owen, then aged sixty-one, sold her rights to the Campobello Company, a group of Americans headed by Alexander S. Porter of Boston, who with a capital of $1,000,000 intended to turn the island into a summer resort. Mrs. Robinson-Owen, her daughter and grandchildren sailed off to England. Her daughter was the wife of Commander Basil Edward Cochrane of the Royal Navy. Fate seemed to have decreed that all the Owens would be sailors or the wives of sailors.

Kate Gannett Wells reserves her most florid prose for her account of an epilogue to the Owen-Campobello saga. In 1890 the island was visited by HMS *Bellerphon* on which Archibald Cochrane, great grandson of the Admiral, was serving as a midshipman. In honour of his visit the Admiral's old cannon fired a salute, and there was a baseball game in the afternoon. She speaks of "the boy's sunny eyes" and "shy frank manner," and tells us that when he came ashore "there was not a man who did not rush forward to greet him." She goes on to say that "this new old friend," this "happy bright boy" expressed "the sure joy of a child who has found again his own," and she gives the back of her hand to the plebeian Yankees in describing how he "waved adieu to those who loved him for his mother's sake with a fondness and pride and sense of personal ownership unknown in 'the States' where ancestry counts for but little."

Obviously Mrs. Wells would have been more than delighted to see a restoration of the Principal Proprietary in the form of young Midshipman Cochrane. One wonders how many of the islanders shared her sentiments.

A MASS MEETING

—OF—

FENIANS!

IRISHMEN, AND
ALL FRIENDS OF LIBERTY!

WILL BE HELD AT

ST. JAMES HALL,

—ON—

Sunday Eve'ng, Oct. 28, 1866

AT HALF PAST 7 O'CLOCK.

Irishmen! The English Government is about to re-enact, on American soil, its deeds of blood. Irish patriots are about to be sacrificed on the altar of English despotism. Can you, will you bear it, or will you rise in your might and trample your enemy in the dust.

Americans! AMERICAN CITIZENS have been condemned to death for treason to a foreign Government. Are our nutralization laws null and void? Has the war of 1812 been fought in vain? Is America to be republican or despotic? Come and answer.

BY ORDER.

Chapter eight ❧ 1866-1867

We're off to capture Canada
For we've nothing else to do.
—from a Fenian marching song

In the meantime Campobello had become the focal point for one of those sequences of events in which the pattern of cause and effect is as giddily improbable as the most unlikely rebound shot ever achieved on a billiards table. In the spring of 1866 an armed body of Irish-Americans determined to seize and occupy the island as a means of harassing their ancestral homeland's ancient enemy, the British. They failed so abysmally that even within their own ranks the attempt came to be known as the "Eastport fizzle." Yet if it had not been for the Fenian Raid it is practically certain that New Brunswick would not have voted that same year to join the Confederation of

British North America, in which case the creation of Canada would have had to be postponed or, quite possibly, abandoned. Without New Brunswick, the Confederation would have consisted of only three colonies — one of them cut off from the others — and it is highly doubtful that it would have been politically, economically and geographically viable.

The Fenian Society was one of a long series of secret revolutionary organizations dedicated to ending England's seven-hundred-year-old ascendancy in Ireland. Many of its members were veterans of the American Civil War that had ended less than a year before their abortive invasion of Campobello. From our vantage point in time, their dream of taking part of British North America hostage for Ireland seems mad enough to have been the brain-child of Don Quixote. But all unsuccessful revolutions seem absurd to posterity. In the context of the times the Fenian strategy was foolhardy but not harebrained. The Fenian ranks included thousands of battle-hardened soldiers, men who had fought at Bull Run and Antietam, while their antagonists would consist largely of ill-trained amateurs, ploughboys and sales clerks, lawyers and farmers — militiamen who had never heard a shot fired in anger. The Fenians had ready access to guns and money. It was not unreasonable to anticipate sympathy if not support from the population of what was to become Canada. (At the time of Confederation, the Irish made up the largest single English-speaking racial bloc in the country; and in 1866 one-third of the inhabitants of New Brunswick were of Irish origin, many of them with bitter memories of English indifference during the great potato famine in Ireland.) More important, they had sound reasons to expect at least passive assistance from the government in Washington, where the traditional belief in the Manifest Destiny of the United States to absorb the entire continent had been reinforced by British support of the now-defeated South. Fenian leaders such as Bernard Doran Killian, the man who plotted and tried to carry out the Campobello expedition, were convinced that Uncle Sam would be delighted to sit back and watch the leprechaun set fire to the lion's tail. Paradoxically, the Fenian movement was motivated by American expansionism as much as by Irish separatism. Killian (at one time an associate of that Father of Confederation D'Arcy McGee) hoped to revive United States claims to Campobello dating back to the American Revolution, besides using the island as a base for raids on British shipping. He had held secret talks in Washington with William Seward, the Secretary of State, and Edwin Stanton, the Secretary of War.

Early in April 1866, more than eight hundred armed Fenians assembled in northeastern Maine, about half of them at Eastport. A ship, the *Ocean Spray*, chartered and loaded with arms in New York, was scheduled to arrive in Passamaquoddy Bay on April 17. But for neither the first nor the last time the Fenians fell victim to what proved in time to be the fatal weakness in the North American branch of their organization. Their ranks were riddled with spies and informers: agents of the British, Upper Canadian and American governments, some of whom had insinuated themselves into the confidence of the topmost leadership. The British government was made aware of the intended Campobello coup so far in advance that it had time to dispatch warships to the scene from as far away as Malta. On April 10, using a tactic that became standard during the era when Britannia ruled the waves, three such warships moved into the mouth of the St. Croix River—and proceeded to engage in gun drill. Two others lay at anchor nearby, and a sixth was on its way. Faced with this disconcerting development, Commandant Killian, who was then in Calais, Maine, did what Irishmen have often

The Fenians, depicted here by cartoonists as a band of drunken bruisers, regarded themselves as soldiers of Ireland.

done under similar circumstances; he made a speech. The Fenian aim, he said, was to obstruct the Confederation of British North America.

The opponents of Confederation in New Brunswick would have preferred a thousand enemies to one friend like Bernard Doran Killian, especially since many of them happened to be Irish Catholics who were even more frightened of being identified with Fenianism than of being swallowed up by the Protestant Upper Canadians. On Saturday, April 14, five Fenians crossed to Indian Island, pointed their revolvers at the customs officer stationed there, and carried off a British flag. To most of the inhabitants of New Brunswick and Maine war appeared to be imminent, and the tension increased with the arrival of two United States gunboats.

Five tense but uneventful days followed. Then the United States government acted. General George C. Meade, the victor of Gettysburg, arrived in Eastport with three hundred soldiers and orders to enforce the Neutrality Act. The Fenians were disarmed and dispersed without a shot being fired. The débâcle had cost them $40,000, the equivalent of at least $250,000 in today's currency. The Fenian threat to Campobello and New Brunswick was over.

Less than a month after the Fenians left Maine a provincial election was held in New Brunswick. Only two years earlier the voters had soundly rejected the pro-Confederation party led by Samuel Leonard Tilley. Now Tilley's supporters claimed that the anti-Confederation party wanted annexation to the United States and dismemberment of the British Empire. An anti-Confederation man, they charged, was only a Fenian in thin disguise. Commenting on Killian's earlier speech, Timothy Anglin, who led the fight against Confederation in his Saint John *Morning Freeman* wrote: "If Mr. Killian were in the pay of the Canadians . . . he could not have said anything better suited to the purposes of the Canadian party." To make it clear that being Irish and Catholic did not necessarily mean that one was in league with the Fenians, members of the hierarchy including Archbishop Thomas Connolly in Halifax and Bishop Colin MacKinnon in Antigonish exerted their influence in support of Confederation, and one of them, James Rogers, the bishop of Chatham, issued a public declaration that it was the duty of the people of New Brunswick to vote for Tilley.

The Fenian bogey was not Tilley's only ally. The Colonial Office in London was on his side, as were the Governor General, the Lieutenant Governor, and the Grand Trunk Railway. Moreover, John A. Macdonald, later Canada's first Prime Minister, had supplied him with $50,000 in Upper Canadian money after receiving a wire in which Tilley told him: "The election can be made certain if the *means* are used." The pro-Confederation party won thirty-three of the forty-one seats in the New Brunswick Legislative Assembly.

In *The Assassination of D'Arcy McGee*, the historian T.P. Slattery said:

> New Brunswick, the province indispensable to Confederation, was now ready, or at least resigned, to enter it. . . . It may well be doubted if this would have ever been the result without the Fenian scare.

The people of Campobello voted overwhelmingly in favour of joining Canada — mainly, so it is said, because their unpopular Principal Proprietary, Captain Robinson-Owen, was a vehement anti-Confederationist.

Chapter nine ❧ 1881-1909

> "Campobello, The Queen of Summer Resorts"
> —heading on an article in The Saint John Daily Sun

"American capital, American enterprise and American culture have laid hold of the little island of Campobello, and with a quickness savouring of the days of Aladdin have transformed the old possessions of Admiral Owen into the most charming watering-place in the world." So wrote an ecstatic reporter for the Saint John *Daily Sun* in July 1882. The reporter went on to quote one Professor N.S. Shaler of Harvard as claiming that "the extensive forests of balsamic firs seem to affect the atmosphere of this region, causing a quiet of the nervous system and inviting sleep." As evidence of this hypothesis the Professor asserted that despite their "hard labour and scanty

diet" the Campobello fisherfolk were "the best conditioned people" he had ever seen and "the children especially" were "models of vigour and health."

Between 1881 and 1883 the new Campobello Company built three hotels: The Owen (erected on the site of the Admiral's house, the house having been moved a short distance away and transformed into a museum and office), the Tyn-y-Coed and the Tyn-y-Maes. The hotels prospered until about 1910. Their advertising brochure described them as being "provided with all the comforts of a refined home" and offering "a quiet and retired life, made wholesome by the soft yet bracing air, never too hot and seldom too cold." It was said that "at Campobello one may find absolute relief from hay fever." Warming to his subject, the brochure writer proclaimed that "the instinct of race bends the American people to the eastern shore. . . . Our people live at high pressure. Here is the

The Tyn-y-Coed and Tyn-y-Maes Hotels, which flourished on Campobello during the heyday of the great summer resorts.

sanitarium, the corrective. Baths of fog are as needful to the senses and the skin as the sun."

The 1880's were the zenith of what Mark Twain christened "the Gilded Age." The United States had been transformed from a remote agrarian republic into one of the world's industrial giants. The frontier had been all but eliminated as railways bound the continent together. Taxes were low and the work ethic was propounded and enforced as if it were a divine ordinance. It was the best of all possible times in which to be rich. The poor, according to economist and sociologist Thorstein Veblen, were quite content to derive such pleasure as they could from observing the rich consume all manner of goods on their behalf. Vicarious consumption, he called it. And among the goods that the rich consumed in vast quantities and with considerable flair was leisure. Presumably they did not feel in need of the moral discipline that work was said

Alexander S. Porter, founder of the Campobello Company, arriving at the Tyn-y-Coed Hotel.

to provide for the poor.

This, for the few who could afford it, was the age of the summer-long vacation, and of the great summer resorts — "the last resorts," as they were called in the title of a book by a historian of the class and period, Cleveland Amory. Those who summered at these places, escaping the heat and dust of such cities as New York, Boston and Montreal, travelled as often as not by private yacht or private railway car. In the end, the resorts fell victim to a variety of factors, including the First World War, the motor car, the servant problem and the income tax.

For the amusement of their guests, the Campobello hotels published a news-sheet called *The Cow Bell*. The issue dated August 20, 1885, lists among the available pastimes: tennis, horseback riding, excursions on the *Admiral*, progressive euchre parties and simply "sitting down in the morning to sew or talk or read."

Other forms of recreation are described in a doggerel verse:

> You return in time for dinner, for here they serve it late,
> And suddenly remember there's a musicale at eight.
> Or perhaps it is a tea party so very Japaneseee
> That you must dress up in costume and help to pass the tea.

An effusion that must surely rank among the worst verses ever written in English, it continues:

> Oh! You who go to Mount Desert, to Newport or to York
> Can you realize that I'm speaking sincerely when I talk
> Of gentlemen outnumbering ladies? Yet 'tis true
> As anyone who's been to Campobello will tell you.

The Cow Bell also found space for gossip:

> The moss-coloured roof of the Roosevelt cottage has excited universal admiration. Its owner is a most accomplished gentleman and can constantly be seen steering his pretty craft amid the islands of the bay.

James and Sara Delano Roosevelt of Hyde Park, New York, first visited Campobello in 1883 when, with their one-year-old son Franklin, they were guests at the Tyn-y-Coed Hotel. They liked the place so well that they bought ten acres of land on a brow overlooking Friar's Bay and erected a fifteen-room "cottage" there — it was ready for occupancy in the summer of 1885. James Roosevelt was Vice President of the Delaware and Hudson Railway. Soon other wealthy Americans built summer homes on the island: Samuel Wells, Dr. Russell Sturgis, Alexander Porter, Gorham Hubbard and Mrs. Hartman Kuhn, of Boston; Travers Cochrane, of Philadelphia; Alfred Pell, of New York; and L.L. Prince, of St. Louis.

The Cow Bell was not the only news-sheet published on Campobello during the 1880's. There was also the *Campobello Jingle*, six issues of which appeared between December 1, 1887, and February 9, 1888. While *The Cow Bell* was aimed at the summer people, the *Jingle*, written in a laboriously droll style, described itself as being the product of a reading club formed "with the object of passing one evening at least a week with pleasure and profit."

The Owen Hotel. At the resorts wealthy Victorian young ladies could meet wealthy Victorian young men.

The following is a typical *Jingle* item:

> In case of any accident happening to our respected butcher, Jabey Pike, we would respectfully suggest the erection of a Mammoth Slaughter and Canning Establishment on the North Road, for the purpose of disposing of the surplus dogs of the island and in case of a meat famine we should then have a reserve of nutritious and tender food, making an agreeable change from the ever present herring.

One of the tacit objectives of the resorts was to provide an opportunity for well-to-do, socially acceptable young women to become acquainted with well-to-do, socially acceptable young men. In July 1886, *Life* magazine (in those pre-Henry Luce days the North American counterpart of *Punch*) printed on its cover a cartoon showing two middle-aged ladies sitting in the lobby of one of the Campobello hotels. The caption read:

> First matron (from Boston): Clara thought the party rather mixed today, but as a rule she is very fond of fishing. Second matron (whose son has been snubbed by Clara): Yes, I see she is on the porch, but not getting very many bites at present.

While the summer people dined (working their way through a menu consisting of celery and olives, soup, fish, sherbet, roast chicken or roast beef, ice cream, cake and nuts), took part in the Grand Annual Ball or attended a "piano recital by Mr. Sigismund Stojowski," the islanders entertained themselves by organizing the Campobello Dramatic Club. Its productions included *Willowdale* (Act 1, The Accusation; Act 2, The Engagement; Act 3, The Wedding); *Red Acres Farm* (Act 1, Driven From Home; Act 2, After the injustices we have had to suffer this night there is murder in my heart; Act 3, same as Act 1 but in winter; Act 4, Return of the prodigal. Forgiven. The mortgage paid. Happy at last); and *Tompkins' Hired Man*

Victorians at play. The members of the Campobello Company picnicking with their wives.

(followed by musical specialities, a club and dumbbell exhibition and a talk on women's suffrage).

There was also a Campobello Debating Society whose stars were John F. Calder and George Byron, the former a fisheries officer and the latter a former King's Printer who was known as the "silver-tongued orator of the Passamaquoddy." Legend has it that at first Calder and Byron refused to allow the young Franklin Roosevelt to join a debating team on the grounds that he was not eloquent enough. They considered his wife Eleanor the better speaker.

John Calder became Roosevelt's close friend. The two first met when the future President was still a child.

It was natural that during his summers on Campobello young Franklin would turn to the island men for adult male companionship. His father was fifty-four when Franklin was born, a dour man who wore muttonchop whiskers, carried a riding crop and was to be described by one of his son's biographers as "an enormous snob." His mother was overprotective and domineering: she kept him in a kilt until he was eight and in short trousers until he was twelve. So the young Franklin, whom nobody ever called Frank, struck up friendships with men like Captain Franklin Calder, Captain Eddie Lank and Captain Shep Mitchell. It was Captain Lank who taught him how to handle a boat and who told him when he was ten years old: "You'll do now. You're a full-fledged seaman, sardine-size." Captain Mitchell later took him on cruises during which he taught him to navigate among the tides, currents, channels and reefs of the Bay of Fundy and Passamaquoddy Bay.

It is even said by some that Roosevelt's famous "Harvard accent" which became familiar to tens of millions through newsreels and radio during the Depression and the Second World War was in reality the accent of the fishermen of Campobello.

Eleanor Roosevelt, whose love for the island was to equal if not exceed that of her husband, visited Campobello for the first time in 1904—a desperately shy and uncertain young woman who had come for the purpose of becoming better acquainted with her future mother-in-law, the imperious and iron-willed Sara. James Roosevelt had died in 1900 while Franklin was in his first year at Harvard. Eleanor was a member of the "Oyster Bay branch" of the Roosevelt family, headed by President Theodore Roosevelt, her uncle, as distinct from the "Hyde Park branch" to which Franklin belonged. They were married in March 1905, and for the next four summers they lived with Sara who, according to Joseph P. Lash in his *Eleanor and Franklin* "managed not only the household but everything else with great firmness." Lash adds that for many years Sara insisted on giving the orders to

the captain of the family yacht, the *Half-Moon*, despite the fact that Franklin was an expert sailor and "only when her son had guests at Campobello was the boat completely turned over to him." Nevertheless, Sara has a defender in Mrs. Linnea Calder who went to work for the Roosevelts when she was thirteen years old. "I think the books have been too hard on Grannie Roosevelt," she says. "Of course she was domineering, but that's how it was in those times." She adds, "And better times they were, too."

In time, and partly as a result of her husband's illness which forced her to summon a degree of energy and initiative that she had not previously known that she possessed, Eleanor Roosevelt was to become a strong personality in her own right, and to play a greater public role than perhaps any other First Lady of the United States. But in those early years she was overawed by her husband, her mother-in-law and life

Fishing boats decorated for a field day.

*Franklin and Eleanor with
two of their children.
Believed to have been taken
in 1918.*

itself. Her lack of self-assurance must have been made more painful by her failure at the athletic activities that Franklin Roosevelt so much enjoyed, such as golf, tennis and skating. However, she was successful in conquering her fear of water, and she learned to fish. Franklin gave his mother an account of a voyage by launch to St. Andrews: " . . . though slightly rough in Passamaquoddy Bay, for a few minutes, Eleanor did not show the least paleness of cheek or tendency to edge toward the rail."

But it was not the custom for wives to accompany their husbands on long cruises. At the end of every summer Eleanor uncomplainingly occupied herself with obtaining provisions for the *Half-Moon* for a voyage to Nova Scotia or Maine —and then, presumably, stood on the dock and waved good-bye to her husband, her elder sons and friends, as a good young wife in those years prior to the First World War was expected to do.

Still, she seems to have been happy. She occupied herself with her small children. She read a great many books. There were guests to entertain. And, as was to be the case throughout her life, there was seldom a time when she was not engaged in some program of self-improvement. One summer she attempted to learn Spanish with the aid of phonograph records, although in the end she had to confess that she might never learn the language "because she still had not mastered the art of making the phonograph work."

Then in 1909 Franklin and Eleanor acquired the first and for a long time the only house that Eleanor could call her own. Previously all the houses in which she and her husband lived had either been rented, or owned, by Sara, who insisted on retaining her grip on the family purse strings. But Mrs. Hartman Kuhn, the owner of the cottage nearest Sara's, had developed an affection for Eleanor equal to that which she had long felt for Franklin. When she died in 1908 her will stipulated that Sara could buy the Kuhn cottage for $5,000—but only on condition that she give it to Franklin and Eleanor. It is this house that is now maintained as the centrepiece of the Roosevelt Campobello International Park.

A home of her own! Eleanor was delighted, of course. The first thing she did was rearrange the furniture in every room in the house.

*A seagull in contemplation.
Wilson's Beach*

Curry's Cove breakwater

East Quoddy lighthouse

Islanders were fascinated discover a landed whale on Wilson's Beach.

Chapter ten ✤ *1910-1920*

While our children were small we went there every summer.... Franklin was always on vacation when he came to Campobello . . . and many of our children's happiest times were with him there.

— Eleanor Roosevelt

Franklin D. Roosevelt Jr. was born on Campobello, a fact that was to be a source of considerable debate many years later when, after he was elected to the United States House of Representatives in a highly publicized upset victory, it was widely believed that he would follow in his father's footsteps and run for President. The United States constitution says that the office can be held only by a native-born citizen, and it has never been made entirely clear what "native-born citizen" means. No longer active in politics but still a frequent visitor to his birthplace as a member of the Roosevelt Campobello International Park Commission, Roosevelt has said : "I think my mother miscalculated, because she intended for me to be born in New York," adding, "but it turned out all right."

The Roosevelts' fourth child and third son was born by the light of an oil lamp in an improvised delivery room in the family cottage on August 17, 1914. In the previous year the father had been appointed Assistant Secretary of the Navy by President Woodrow Wilson, a job he was to hold throughout the First World War despite his periodic attempts to persuade Wilson to allow him to resign and become a naval officer. When it became evident that Eleanor was about to have her baby, Franklin set off in the *Half-Moon* to fetch a doctor from Lubec. By the time the doctor arrived the baby had been delivered by the Roosevelts' housekeeper. Franklin and Eleanor's other children were Anna, James, Elliot and John.

The future President's political career had begun in 1910, when he won for the Democrats a seat in the New York state senate that had been held by the Republicans for twenty-two years. Although the time that Roosevelt himself was free to spend at Campobello was greatly reduced after he became Assistant Secretary of the Navy, Eleanor and the children were usually there during July, August and part of September.

F.D.R. Jr. recalls the excitement of his boyhood trips to the island:

> We came up usually in time for the fourth of July. It was a two-day trip in those days. We took the train from Hyde Park into New York city and that was quite an expedition. Then we spent the night in Boston and boarded the Boston and Maine Railway the next day. We usually took a whole car for each day of the trip. There was a wonderful little train that came down to Eastport — pulled by one of those old wood-burning steam engines. Sometimes we were allowed to go up and sit with the engineer and fireman. That was very exciting for a small boy, watching the fireman throw those big logs into the furnace that

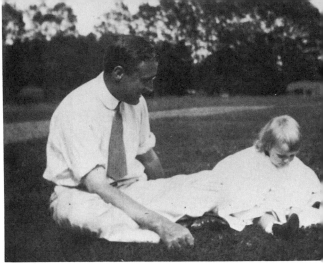

kept the steam going. We would stop at all the little stations. The Indians would come aboard and sell us their little birchbark toy canoes and their moccasins. Then we would be met at Eastport by horses and carriages and a big wagon for the baggage. We'd be taken down to the dock where Captain Calder would be waiting in his boat. He'd take us across the water to our place, and there would be a big race up the hill to see who could get to the house the fastest. It was a wonderful, happy feeling when we finally got there.

It was here on Campobello, reports F.D.R. Jr., that the "bunch of wild Indians" that were the Roosevelt children learned to play tennis and golf and handle boats. The children went on hayrides and picnics with their mother, and walked along the cliffs with their father. "It was a test of our ability to jump from rock to rock and not fall into the Bay of Fundy." Young Franklin and John rode bareback on draft horses and went up to Friar's Head to lasso sheep with a stolen clothesline. "That's where I learned for the first time that sheep would bite." On Sundays they marched to St. Anne's Church. "[In the family pew] my father would sit on the end and next to him would be my grandmother — that was the pecking order in our family." Food was kept in an old-

The Roosevelt yacht, the Half-Moon, in 1913.

F.D.R. with his son Elliot in 1912.

fashioned ice box which F.D.R. Jr. claims was more efficient than the modern refrigerator, in that its contents were actually cooler when the door of the box was opened than when it was shut. "You forget how good the living was before all of these modern gadgets." When it was time for lunch Eleanor would go out on the porch and bellow down to the water through a megaphone. "I can hear her voice now. We'd all come running up the hill." There were no fences. "Early in the morning, up the road would come the cows with a young boy or girl driving them. Then in the evening they would be driven home to be milked. It was very charming and I suppose very much like the Swiss villages."

The Roosevelt family at Campobello, 1912.

There was no telephone in the Roosevelt cottage until 1933. "They would send somebody up from the village, and we would have to go down on a bicycle or walk, and put the answering call through from there. One telephone on the whole island!"

While the Assistant Secretary of the Navy's visits were fewer and briefer than in the past they were more dramatic. He delighted in being able to order a battleship, the U.S.S.

North Dakota, to take part in the Independence Day celebrations at Eastport in 1913. It was characteristic of him that although he boarded the ship informally dressed in summer flannels he had previously arranged with the captain for the battleship to give him the seventeen-gun salute to which his office entitled him.

Eleanor's feelings about the *North Dakota*'s visit were mixed, since she was called upon to entertain the ship's officers with teas, dinners and card games. "I could hardly bear that much excitement again," she wrote to her husband, after hearing it suggested that he might come back in August with a flotilla. He assured her that no more battleships were coming. "I may come up with a destroyer later, but that means only three officers."

When in Campobello, Roosevelt worried about not being in close enough touch with developments affecting the department of the navy. "As soon as I go away we seem to land marines somewhere," he wrote to the head of the department, Josephus Daniels. On the other hand, when he was in Washington he worried about his wife and children. In 1917, for instance, he decided that although there was a "500 to 1 chance against the possibility," it was conceivable that a German submarine might attack Campobello. He warned Eleanor that if a U-boat came into the bay and began to shell Eastport or Welshpool he wanted her to "grab the children and beat it into the woods," and he added that he was not joking.

There had been a different and less fanciful fear in the summer of 1916. The United States had been afflicted with the worst epidemic of infantile paralysis in its history and Roosevelt was terrified that his children would catch the disease. At the cottage he spent hours killing the flies that were believed to carry the infection. And when he returned to Washington he wrote Eleanor: "Please kill all the flies I left. I think it really important."

In 1920 Roosevelt was the Democratic candidate for the United States Vice Presidency on a ticket headed by an Ohio newspaperman, James M. Cox. The Cox-Roosevelt ticket was defeated by a margin of almost two to one by a Republican slate headed by another Ohio newspaperman, Warren G. Harding, whose running mate was "Silent Cal" Coolidge. A historian of the campaign was to write that the Republicans who pledged a "return to normalcy" won because the American people were "tired from the suffering and bloodshed" of the First World War and wanted "to be let alone, to sleep in the sun."

Out of politics for the first time in ten years, Roosevelt became a Wall Street lawyer and vice president in charge of the New York office of the Fidelity and Deposit Company of Maryland.

Except for brief, hurried visits he had been away from Campobello for a long time. He decided to go there for his first real vacation since before the war.

Chapter eleven ❧ *1921-1933*

The world was lucky to see him born.

— refrain of a song written by
Woody Guthrie following President
Roosevelt's death

When the 140-foot power yacht *Sebalo* arrived in Welshpool harbour one foggy August day in 1921 Roosevelt was at the helm. During the voyage from New York harbour to Campobello on the yacht owned by his business associate Van Lear Black he had stood at the wheel hour after hour, guiding the craft northeastward past Frenchman Bay and Machias Bay, into Grand Manan Channel and through the dangerous Lubec Narrows. The weather was rough, with impenetrable fog and a turbulent sea, and Roosevelt was the only man aboard who knew these waters. When the Narrows made Black (himself a seasoned yachtsman) nervous, Roosevelt told him how he had once steered a high-speed destroyer through this same strait, to the surprise and relief of its commander, a young Lieutenant named William Halsey Jr. (Years later when time had transformed that young Lieutenant into Admiral "Bull" Halsey, Commander-in-Chief of the Third Pacific Fleet, he too recalled how a "white-flannelled yachtsman" had taken his ship through that menacing channel, and commented that Roosevelt "really knew his business.")

Among the crowd waiting on the dock in Welshpool were Eleanor, his "dearest Babs," and their five children, "the Chicks." Also waiting there was Roosevelt's right-hand man, Louis Howe, an asthmatic gnome who boasted that he was one of the four ugliest men in New York, and of whom a historian was to write that he was so close to Roosevelt that "to a limited but important degree there was a virtual fusion of identities to create a double self."

That night the Roosevelts and their guests watched the fishermen seining the weir that extended out into the sea from the Roosevelt shoreline. Summoned by a watchman's horn, the fishermen in rubber boots, heavy sweaters and sou'westers, drew up their nets full of seething herring and emptied them into small boats by the reddish light of flares. It looked like the pictures in Bible stories, Eleanor said.

The following morning Roosevelt was out of bed at day-break. During the voyage from New York he had told his friends that he would take them fishing in the Bay of Fundy. The fog had lifted and it was a fine, clear day. They boarded the Sebalo's motor tender and went out on the bay to fish for cod.

He would bait their hooks, of course. No doubt he enjoyed playing the role of the salty islander initiating a pack of land-lubbers into the mysteries of the sea: like many men with an insatiable appetite for life he had a deep love of the theatrical gesture. As the sun rose higher the day got hotter. In baiting the hooks it was necessary for Roosevelt to keep walking back and forth on a narrow plank that passed close to the tender's engine. By noon he was drenched in sweat. Then his foot slipped and he fell overboard. He was to recall years later that he had "never felt anything so cold as that water." In seconds he was back on board, laughing with the others at this joke at his expense. He continued to wear his wet clothes until they were dried by the sun and the heat of the engine.

Later that afternoon when they returned to the cottage he found that he felt vaguely uncomfortable: sluggish and with a dull ache in his bones. But he did not take this seriously. He had been schooled to drive his body to the limits of its endurance. Rather than convincing him that he ought to rest, his sense of discomfort only made him more determined to exert himself. If he was out of shape, well, that meant he had been spending too much of his time behind a desk. He would solve that problem now that he was back on Campobello.

The pace set by Roosevelt was too hectic for his guests from New York. Soon they were exhausted from trying to keep up with him. Conveniently, telegrams began to arrive with word of business transactions that made it imperative for the recipient to leave the island at once. The *Sebalo* sailed away, leaving the Roosevelts, the Howes and a few other guests who were virtually members of the Roosevelt family. But the feverish activity never slackened.

Roosevelt took the smaller children sailing on his 24-foot sloop the *Vireo* which he had bought he said so that the boys could learn to sail as he had done. He played tennis with the older children. After supper they all played baseball. The nearest he came to resting was when he and Louis Howe worked on model boats or discussed their plans for his bid for the governorship of New York State in 1922.

On August 10 the family had been sailing on the *Vireo* for hours and were bound for home when they sighted a forest fire on a small island and went ashore to fight it—beating at the flames with evergreen boughs until their eyes were bleary with smoke and, as Roosevelt later recalled, they were "begrimed, smarting with spark-burns, exhausted."

The future President then insisted that everyone get into a bathing suit and jog two miles for a swim in Lake Glensevern. Before they jogged back to the cottage, Roosevelt in accordance with his usual custom topped off his swim in the relatively warm waters of the lake with an icy plunge into the bay.

His dip did not refresh him as it usually did; and back at the cottage he found that he was too tired to dress. He sat on the porch in his wet bathing suit and read the day's mail.

When he began shivering violently he decided that he had caught a cold. He told Eleanor that he had best not eat with the others for fear of infecting them. He would go to bed, and she could send up a tray.

But despite his long day of strenuous exercise he discovered that he had no appetite and could not really sleep. Franklin Jr. recalls how "in the middle of that night he tried to go to the bathroom but he couldn't stand up, so my mother woke up and he was crawling on his hands and knees to the bathroom." The next morning when he got out of bed to shave he found that his left leg dragged.

It was nothing, he told his daughter Anna when she brought up his breakfast, only lumbago and a touch of fever. But before long his left leg would not move at all and by afternoon his right leg was equally powerless.

An islander was dispatched to the mainland in a motor launch to fetch the family's summer physician, Dr. E. H. Bennett of Lubec. His diagnosis was an unusually heavy cold. But

Roosevelt, whose temperature had risen to 102 degrees, was not convinced. "I don't know what's the matter with me, Louis," he kept saying to Howe, his face white and twisted with worry and pain.

By August 12 the weakness and pain had spread to his shoulders, arms and fingers. It was decided that another doctor ought to be called in. Bennett and Howe went to Lubec and telephoned the various resorts. They learned that Dr. William W. Keen, a nationally known medical man from Philadelphia, was vacationing at Bar Harbour. He was contacted and agreed to come to the island and spend a night at the cottage.

After examining the patient, Dr. Keen decided that "a clot of blood from a sudden congestion had settled in the lower spinal cord temporarily removing the power to move although not the power to feel." He recommended massage.

The massaging, which Roosevelt found almost unbearably painful, was undertaken by Eleanor and Howe. During the first two weeks of his illness these two were his only nurses. Eleanor slept on a couch in his room. Roosevelt's wife and his Man Friday who had not previously been close now found in their love and concern for him the basis for life-long friendship. As he became almost completely helpless and sank into deeper despair it was their joint task to care for his every bodily need and to strengthen his waning will to survive.

Roosevelt would one day confess to a close friend and colleague that during those black August days as he lay there staring at the wallpaper with its yellow flowers and green leaves his despair became absolute. He was convinced that God had forsaken him.

On August 25 there arrived a specialist in orthopedics from Newport, Dr. Robert D. Lovett.

His diagnosis — which proved to be the correct one — was

infantile paralysis.

Polio.

Once he knew the name and nature of his antagonist, Roosevelt recovered his fighting spirit. His body was still powerless and in pain but now his indomitable will was once again in operation. He and his comrades-in-arms, Eleanor and Howe, seemed determined to pretend that this poliomyelitis was only a bad joke, an accident different only in degree and not in kind from his plunge from the *Sebalo*'s motor tender into the frigid Bay of Fundy. There was laughter in the sickroom as was remarked by Roosevelt's mother when she returned from a trip to Europe. And to Eleanor's relief Sara joined in the game, although as Eleanor afterwards wrote, "I am sure that, out of sight, she wept many hours" for her "poor Franklin" of whose pathetic crippled legs she had once been "so proud."

Roosevelt left Campobello on September 13. Arrangements had been made to have a private railway car transport him from Eastport to New York. His old friend Captain Franklin Calder improvised a stretcher on which he and several other islanders carried the patient down to the motorboat. On the mainland the stretcher was loaded on a luggage cart, taken to the train and passed through a window. Although Captain Calder and the others were as gentle as possible the journey was sheer agony for Roosevelt.

Louis Howe, mindful even under these desperate circumstances of his friend's political career and resolved not to allow that career to be damaged by public awareness of the full extent of Roosevelt's paralysis, managed to trick the reporters waiting in Eastport so that none of them was present when Roosevelt was put aboard the train.

"Isn't it wonderful to think how bravely and hopefully he is facing it all?" Captain Calder wrote to Eleanor.

In his book *F.D.R.: The Beckoning of Destiny 1882-1928*, Kenneth S. Davis writes: "Of greater life-affirming courage and fortitude in a political leader of the first rank, all history affords few examples." The climax of the Davis book, as of the Dore Schary film *Sunrise at Campobello*, is Roosevelt's triumphant walk across the platform to the podium at the Democratic national convention in Houston in 1928 where he stood—his leg braces hidden from the audience, his left hand gripping the lectern while his right acknowledged the applause—to nominate Al Smith for President.

Some 15,000 persons saw and heard him that day, while 15,000,000 others listened to him on the radio. He had practised for that speech—and more especially for that walk—until he was adept at hiding the fact that his left leg was still almost useless. The son who walked beside him had been schooled to keep smiling broadly as his grinning father grasped his arm tightly or suddenly leaned heavily against him.

Five years later Roosevelt was in the White House. After his death Eleanor was to write: "Franklin's illness was another turning point, and proved a blessing in disguise; for it gave him the strength and courage he had not had before. He had to think out the fundamentals of living and learn the greatest of all lessons—infinite patience and never-ending persistence."

The Roosevelts cruising from Marion, Massachusetts, to Campobello, on Amberjack II *in 1933.*

Chapter twelve ❧ The Park

It is most fitting that the memory of so gallant and illustrious an American should be honoured on the Canadian island which he loved.

— Queen Elizabeth, the Queen Mother

Franklin D. Roosevelt Jr. says that his father did not often visit Campobello in later years, not only because of lack of time but also because "subconsciously or perhaps consciously but unexpressed," he was afraid of returning as a cripple to a place where he had so often walked, run, ridden horseback or gone cliff-climbing. After his attack of polio he did not return to the island for twelve years. On the night of his election to the Presidency, the people of Campobello celebrated by building a bonfire of barrels that could be seen from twenty miles away. Then, on June 29, 1933, he sailed into Welshpool at the helm of the yacht *Amberjack II*, escorted by a cruiser and two destroyers and accompanied by his mother, his wife and three of his sons. F.D.R. Jr. recalls how the crowd at the wharf momentarily stopped cheering as they watched the President being lifted from the cockpit of the yacht and into a waiting car. Few of them had realized how helpless he was. When the cheering resumed, it was louder than before. "Many of the old fishermen whom he had known as a boy turned out to welcome him. He really got a great kick out of it."

Next day the Roosevelts invited half the island to a picnic. Erlon Cline, eighty-five, likes to tell the story of how he was ordered off the beach behind the Roosevelt cottage by a Secret Service man, after having been hired to clean it before the arrival of the picnickers. "I said to him, 'You got a gun and I got a fork, it looks like a saw-off, don't it?' Afterwards I told the President about it, and he threw back his head and laughed in that way he had, and he said to me, 'Erlon, you did right; always hold your ground'."

Erlon Cline. "Always hold your ground, Erlon," Presi[dent] Roosevelt said.

As President, Roosevelt actively encouraged a project conceived by an old Campobello neighbour. There had come to the island in 1919 an American engineer, Dexter P. Cooper, who was recuperating from an illness after working in Russia and South America, as well as in the United States. He developed a plan for using the tides to generate electric power, through the construction of a system of dams and sea-gates and the creation of two great basins, one in Passamaquoddy Bay and one in Maine's Cobscook Bay. When the moon's pull is strongest, the tides at the head of the Bay of Fundy may rise and fall as much as fifty-three feet. In 1935, Roosevelt allocated $10-million in relief funds to the project and sent 3,000 relief workers to prepare the site, but the effort had to be abandoned a year later when Congress refused to advance further funds. The plan was opposed by Canadian fishing interests and rejected by United States engineers as too remote and expensive.

Roosevelt made two more brief visits to Campobello, one in 1936 and the other in 1939. His biographers record that in the last months of his life when he was sick and exhausted he frequently startled his associates by suddenly introducing into the conversation some small and long past incident on The Outer Island.

On August 1, 1946, about a year and a half after his death, the Historic Sites and Monuments Board of Canada erected a red granite cairn and bronze tablet at Welshpool. The plaque reads:

> In happy memory of Franklin Delano Roosevelt, 1882-1945, statesman and humanitarian who, during many years of his eventful life, found in this tranquil island, rest, refreshment and freedom from care. To him it was always the "beloved island."

The Campobello cottage went to Roosevelt's son Elliot, who sold it to the Hammer brothers, Armand, Harry and Victor of New York. Three months before her death in 1962, Eleanor, who was already very sick, spent five days as a guest of the new owners. She was driven to the East Quoddy lighthouse, to Herring Cove and to other places that she had known and loved for more than half a century. Afterwards she wrote to her hosts: "I am leaving much stronger than I came and attribute the renewal of my strength to the peace and quiet I found here."

East Quoddy lighthouse.

Her health had prevented her from attending an event that took place during the same month as her final visit to the island — the official opening by her son James of the Roosevelt International Bridge, linking the island with Lubec, Maine. Not everybody regarded the bridge as an unmixed blessing. Said Erlon Cline sadly: "Campobello isn't an island any more."

Nevertheless, the bridge emphasized what President John F. Kennedy called the "bond of friendship" between Canada

and the United States. Not long after the bridge had been opened, Kennedy, speaking at Brunswick, Maine, proposed that the ties "be further strengthened" by the establishment of an international park at the Roosevelt summer home. The Hammer brothers, who already had restored the cottage to something like its original condition, donated the property to the governments of the two countries.

The first steps toward creation of the Roosevelt Campobello International Park were taken on May 11, 1963, at a meeting between Prime Minister Lester B. Pearson and President Kennedy. The park was then established on January 22, 1964, by an agreement signed on behalf of their respective countries by President Lyndon B. Johnson and Prime Minister Pearson. A joint statement declared:

"Campobello's not an island any more." The Roosevelt International Bridge connects Lubec, Maine, left, to Campobello, right.

The establishment of the Roosevelt Campobello International Park represents a unique example of international co-operation. The park will stand forever as an expression of the close relationship between Canada and the United States as well as a fitting memorial to the President of the United States who so greatly strengthened that relationship and who himself spent so many happy hours of rest and relaxation on Canadian soil and in Canadian waters.

The Park's Tourist Information Centre and rest area.

Epilogue

"Fishing?" Johnnie Malloch says. "Yes, they call it a trade nowadays, I guess. It used to be just something that we did to keep from starving to death." He traps lobsters in season, works a herring weir and goes handlining for cod and pollock, which means that he works close to home. His brother Roy, on the other hand, used to work on the purse seiners that go as far away as Newfoundland and stay for as long as three weeks, their crews of up to six men being paid according to the size of the catch. Both the weirmen and the boatmen are specialists, unlike their forefathers who not only fished but farmed and, when they were short of cash, went off to the

John Malloch, lobsterman, weir-
man, boat man and man of
Campobello.

Roy Malloch and his son Calvin,
both good men at handlining
pollock.

mainland to be loggers and mill hands. Only a generation
ago, the cattle and sheep roamed where they pleased, and the
wooden boats were powered by second-hand automobile en-
gines. The boats of today, purse seiners that fish for herring
and draggers that fish for haddock, cod and pollock, are up to
more than one hundred feet long and equipped with electronic echo sounders, radar and ship-to-shore radiophones.
Nobody farms, and there are few vegetable gardens. Those
who are not fishermen work in the sardine factory or the
fish-packing plant.

Everything is better today, in the opinion of Earle C. Dinsmore, seventy-nine years old and for thirty-five years a lighthouse keeper. "When I came here in 1918 conditions were
disgraceful." He says proudly that he had the first bathroom,
the first electricity and the first radio on Campobello, and he
scoffs at those who romanticize the past.

Asa and Zelma Brown. "Man, dear, I done it all. There ain't no fishin' I did never done."

Earl Dinsmore, who believes that everything is better today.

Not every older resident agrees. Asa Brown, eighty-four, says, "Today we're livin' better than the rich people did seventy years ago," but he adds that the island is not so neighbourly as it was when he was young. "The world's gone crazy over money." He is Campobello's most renowned talker but on the page his words are like the lyrics of a song without the music. Like all the islanders, his speech depends to an extraordinary degree on timing, intonation, facial expression, gesture and, most subtle of all, on implication: what is said is often less meaningful than what is deliberately left unsaid. "I've done it all," he says. "Man, I've worked all the days of my life; there ain't no fishin' I did never done." He speaks of the electronic sounders and the nets made of "plastic or some other damned thing. The fish don't have much of a chance, now do he?" It is plain that he respects the fish and even sympathizes with them.

"One of them biology fellas came over from the mainland," he says. "He told me he had eighteen men under him. I told him I used to have three hundred men under me. I was caretaker in a cemetery." He is still prepared to climb up and down a thirty-five-foot ladder at the breakwater, and work all day cutting herring into bait for the long lines used in trawling for haddock. When he and his wife Zelma talk with a stranger, one will begin a sentence and let the other end it, or will purposely hesitate so that the other can insert a word and thereby give it an added emphasis.

Both Asa and Zelma had a brother who was drowned. Landsmen invariably express astonishment when they learn that most Campobello fishermen have never learned to swim. Men like Johnnie Malloch reply that the water in which they work is paralyzingly cold, and when the sea is so rough that a man cannot be rescued immediately a swimmer will survive for only a few minutes longer than a non-swimmer. Few landsmen are prepared to accept that explanation; they say the fishermen are fatalists: the sea cannot be that lethal. Johnnie Malloch shrugs, "I hope they never have to find out."

At the moment, one of Johnnie Malloch's rubber-booted feet rests on the gunwhale of a dory that floats on its side rather than its bottom, the other kicks the upright stakes of the weir to propel him forward as he draws in a seine net seething with herring. A half-dozen small boats are tied up outside the fenced, roughly circular trap, together with the vessel that will carry the bulk of his catch to the sardine factory — "sardine" being in North America simply another name for a small herring. Malloch and the onlookers, most of whom have come to buy bait, exchange chaff.

"Hey, I don't need any help from you, Roy."

"Well, Johnnie, one of these days you may catch enough fish that you will."

The boats contain males of all ages, all of whom know one another intimately. To the men, the little boys are distinct personalities, to be addressed by name. As the purse seine surfaces the fish are pumped aboard the sardine carrier by suction. As they pass through the loading machinery, their scales are scraped off and dumped into a separate container, to be sold to a manufacturer of artificial pearls. The air smells of fish, salt, tar, diesel oil and sweat. Overhead the gulls circle and dive, their cries like mocking laughter.

It develops that today the cannery can accept only a part of the Malloch catch; the rest must wait in the weir. The men are careful in handling the net that contains the leftover fish. "You're out of luck if any of them die; if there are dead fish in your weir you might as well tear it down."

A seal has been damaging the weirs. "If it doesn't stop tormentin' us I guess we'll just have to shoot him," Johnnie Malloch says. His tone is almost affectionate.

When we return to shore, Malloch shows us an old-fashioned instrument for locating and estimating the size of schools of fish. It is simply a weight attached to a line. You drop the weight in the water and let your fingers assess the movements of the line as the fish bump against it. "Takes a while to get the knack of it," he says. His father has told him of a time when Campobello men located fish at night from the phosphorescence of their bodies just below the surface. "But there's too much artificial light for that now, even on Campobello." Then: "Now I want to show you a baby I'm really proud of." And he brings out an electronic sounder about the size of a car battery. "Of course, this is nothing compared to what they have on the draggers, that's like science fiction."

We go out again to where men and boys, among them Johnnie's brother Roy and Roy's son Calvin, are handlining. "Maybe we can catch a pollock for supper," Johnnie says.

Campobello fishermen, unlike their Newfoundland counter-parts, generally do not eat cod, not because they dislike it but because they are always plentifully supplied with species of fish they like better. One of the most popular island dishes is Corned Pollock, which consists simply of fresh pollock, heavily salted and left overnight, then boiled in the same pot with potatoes, and served with side dishes of shruncheons (scraps of fat salt pork fried to a crisp), onion slices soaked in vinegar and an egg sauce.

The handliners go out for a little way, throw out their lines, then switch off their motors and drift in towards the shore. Men call to one another across the water, using nicknames that they have borne since childhood, exchanging jokes so familiar to all of them that they need catch only a word or two before they laugh.

I think of the high school students we talked with, whose gathering place is on the corner opposite the post office in Wilson's Beach, where they sit on a fence and like kids all over the continent wait for something to happen. All the girls said they wanted to leave the island. Half the boys said they would like to stay. A fourteen-year-old boy explained, "You see, we got the boats, but they got nothin'."

Back on shore again without having caught our supper, we are introduced to Walton Malloch, eighty-six-year-old father of Johnnie and Roy, who sits on an old car seat in the shade beside a shed, where he can watch the fishermen. He grins at these landsmen who have gone to watch men seine a herring weir as if it were not a job of work but a show. "I've seen the herring so thick they rolled up on the shore," he says. "That was a long time ago." He was struck by lightning twice, his wife tells us. Both times he was out in a boat. "For a second or two I thought it had blown my head off," he chuckles. Mrs. Malloch says that on nights when he was fishing she would put the children to bed and sit, propped up with pillows, knitting until she fell asleep. I remember the fisherman's wife on the neighbouring island of Grand Manan who, when she was asked if the foghorn situated near her home kept her from sleeping, answered that she never heard it except on nights when her man was out on the bay.

As we stand beside their century-old house, saying our goodbyes, Mrs. Malloch points to houses that belong to her children and grandchildren. It seems that every house within sight is occupied by her descendants.

"I suppose you've heard a lot of stories about the Owen family," I say to them hopefully.

Mr. and Mrs. Malloch look at each other, anxious to please but baffled. "No," Walton Malloch says at last, "I can't say we ever knew anybody by that name around here."

Johnnie returns us to the Roosevelt Campobello International Park. We walk down the forest path between the Roosevelt and Prince cottages to the shores of Friar's Bay. The Prince cottage has white-columned porches with miniature hanging gardens. It is already dark under the fir and spruce boughs but when we reach the beach we emerge into the light of the sunset. The wild strawberries growing at the edge of the woods are beginning to ripen. Yesterday Zelma Brown informed us incredulously that some of the tourists claimed they had never before seen wild strawberries, and Asa said how that was nothing: some of them couldn't tell a mackerel from a haddock or their left hand from their right.

To our right and some little distance away stands Welshpool, with its wharf, and beyond it, high on a cliff, Admiral Owen's white Man O' War House. To our left, across the water and towards the sun, stands Friar's Head, the great black stone that resembles a monk deep in contemplation. The British sailors who used the Friar for gunnery practice during the War of 1812 never succeeded in knocking off its head. It is so timeless here at this moment that David Owen, that irascible scholar and bitter exile, might almost step out from the shadows behind us and demand to know what the devil we are doing on his land. Or perhaps on the back lawn of the Roosevelt cottage, hidden from us by the trees, young women were only this afternoon playing tennis in great floppy hats and in skirts that hung within two or three inches of the ground, and this evening there will be a sing-song in which we will gather with the other summer people around the piano in the living room of the cottage, the men in detachable collars and cuffs and the women in bustles and whalebone corsets, and join in the singing of such current popular favourites as *My Gal Sal* and *The Banks of the Wabash*.

The only sounds are the whistling of birds and the splash of the waves that throw themselves downward on the shore like exhausted swimmers.

Appendix

ORIGINAL ROOSEVELT CAMPOBELLO PARK COMMISSION – 1964

AMERICAN MEMBERS

Edmund S. Muskie,
  Chairman
Franklin D. Roosevelt, Jr.
Sumner T. Pike

CANADIAN MEMBERS

D. Leo Dolan,
  Vice-Chairman
Robert A. Tweedie
Murray J. Johnston

ALTERNATES

Samuel Rosenman
Grace Tully
Harry Umphrey

Donald A. McLean
Alice Howe
Stuart Trueman

ROOSEVELT CAMPOBELLO PARK COMMISSION-1975

AMERICAN MEMBERS

Edmund S. Muskie,
  Vice-Chairman
Franklin D. Roosevelt, Jr.
Curtis Hutchins

CANADIAN MEMBERS

Hédard J. Robichaud,
  Chairman
David Walker
Robert A. Tweedie

ALTERNATES

James Rowe
Grace Tully
Lawrence Stuart

Stuart Trueman
Brenda Norris
Roland Frazee

FORMER MEMBER AND CHAIRMAN

Alan Macnaughton

HONORARY MEMBER

Sumner T. Pike

Photo credits

The author and publisher gratefully acknowledge the invaluable assistance of the staff of the Roosevelt Campobello International Park and many of the people of Campobello in gathering together the illustrations in this book.

The author and publisher also wish to thank the following individuals and organizations for the illustrations listed below.

Clifford Hodgson: 4; 51; 67; 117; all colour photographs with the exception of the whale on the beach

Franklin D. Roosevelt Library: 90; 98; 103 (both); 104; 114

New Brunswick Dept. of Tourism: 68 (both); 118 right (Harvey Studios, Calais, Maine); 120

Campobello Library Assn., New Brunswick Museum (J. Hinson): 3; 17; 57; 71; 77 (regulations)

Linnea Calder: 72

Public Archives of Canada: 20 and 28 (both by R. Short, courtesy Historical Services & Consultants Ltd., Toronto); 43 (J. D. Kelly)

New Brunswick Museum: 30 (Webster Canadiana Collection); 66; 119; 128

Hazel Calder: 106

New Brunswick Travel Bureau, Fredericton: 118 left (Clifford Hodgson)

Nova Scotia Information Service: 11; 69

The Harvey Studios Ltd., Fredericton: Appendix

Ontario Archives: 82

Royal Ontario Museum, Dept. of Archeology: 9

Senator Edward Muskie: 59; colour photo of landed whale

Roosevelt Campobello International Park: 5; 76; 77; 92; 93; 95; 97

Campobello Library, Welshpool: 33; 51; 62
J. Hinson: 8; 116; 122; 123

The publisher welcomes any information which will enable him, in subsequent editions, to correct any errors made in giving credit lines.